Down East Delicious

175
Recipes from
MAINE
KITCHENS

Sandra Oliver

Down East Books
CAMDEN, MAINE

Down East Books

An imprint of The Globe Pequot Publishing Group, Inc.
64 South Main Street
Essex, CT 06426
www.globepequot.com

Distributed by NATIONAL BOOK NETWORK

Copyright © 2024 by Sandra Oliver

British Library Cataloguing in Publication Information available

Library of Congress Cataloging-in-Publication Data is available
ISBN 9781684752041 (cloth) | ISBN 9781684752058 (ebook)

♾™ The paper used in this publication meets the minimum requirements of American National Standard for Information Sciences—Permanence of Paper for Printed Library Materials, ANSI/NISO Z39.48-1992.

Contents

Contents

Introduction

In April 2005, I began writing a weekly column called Taste Buds for the *Bangor Daily News*. In April 2023, nine hundred and thirty-six recipes later (with maybe a dozen repeats), on its eighteenth anniversary, I stopped writing Taste Buds.

Mildred "Brownie" Schumpf, whose *BDN* recipe column ran for forty-something years, and Marjorie Standish, who wrote weekly for twenty years for the *Maine Sunday Telegram,* both created cookbook compilations of their columns. Following their footsteps, I authored *Maine Home Cooking* in 2012, published by Down East with one hundred and seventy-five recipes. And now here is *Down East Delicious* with another assortment of some of my favorite and most useful recipes collected since 2012.

To be perfectly honest, I don't particularly like writing recipes. What I do like—actually love—is having conversations with column readers who have shared their recipes with me along with all the stories and memories associated with them. I am the lucky and grateful recipient of much kitchen wisdom from Mainers all over DownEast, neighbors and friends nearby, to Mainers living in farther reaches of the country who stay in touch with their home state. I don't miss a weekly deadline very much; I do miss hearing from folks and perhaps this book will seem a little like a reunion of old friends. At least, it will put some helpful recipes in your hands again or, perhaps, for the first time.

STORY AND HISTORY

Having spent a few decades exploring and writing about food history, I have always gravitated toward the backstory of our food. When a recipe comes along with a beguiling family tale attached or reveals some detail about what this dish meant in the past, I bite on it hard. Cooking a recipe from the past is a little bit of time travel; sometimes it is a little like sitting down at the kitchen table with an ancestor, your own or someone else's. We honor them and their accomplishments by recording their recipes.

Mainly, I think we all like stories, and even if you don't cook you might enjoy reading this cookbook as a work of non-fiction.

THESE ARE YOUR RECIPES

The majority of these recipes came from column readers, sometimes in response to my query in the paper, sometimes because something they read triggered a memory. And because a weekly column can turn a writer into a kind of recipe predator to satisfy the weekly need for something to write about, sometimes, I cornered friends at potlucks or dinners to collect a recipe.

I owe each recipe contributor a huge vote of thanks. You have been so generous all these years.

Because, as a home cook like you, I don't have vats of time to fiddle around in the kitchen and can't be running off to the store at the drop of a hat for some missing ingredient, I value recipe tinkerbility: adjustable for substitution, or omission; for suiting personal taste; accommodating food allergies or avoidance among those around the dining table.

Some of the best recipes will simply absorb an array of leftovers or miscellaneous ingredients to use up before they spoil. Some of the best recipes aren't recipes, but are ideas, or a set of suggestions. Sam Sifton of the *New York Times* Cooking Section calls them "No Recipe Recipes." You probably already cook like this from time to time.

HEARING FROM YOU

Between 2005 and 2023, one great shift occurred in how we communicated. In the early days, I received recipes in the mail, sometimes written on handy recipe cards, sometimes on notepaper. In the past ten years, most have come by email. When recipes came in envelopes, the return address told me where the recipe donor lived. If the recipe came by email, if I didn't remember to ask, I often didn't know the cook's location which is why you may read a name without a hometown identified.

RECIPE EXTINCTION

The internet and YouTube are full of cooks whose recipes depend on pre-made items which can be assembled to make a dessert or casserole. Quite possibly this is delicious, and the recipe will serve until the product is reformulated or eliminated in favor of the next great thing.

Some common products, like chocolate chips, no longer work as they did before as manufacturers reformulate them to use less expensive ingredients. Then there is the great shrinkage problem as producers periodically shave off a few ounces so that a can or package looks the same but instead of holding sixteen ounces, now contains fifteen, or thirteen and a half. So it goes. Sooner or later an old, favorite family recipe no longer tastes the same, or makes the quantity it used to. If it is irreplicable, it goes extinct.

In this cookbook, I've tried to keep to a minimum of recipes relying on pre-packaged ingredients both so that you will be able to make the dish well into the future, and so you can avoid the wasteful packaging that come with prepared foods, and since the prepared food often costs more than the ingredients would cost purchased separately, cooking from scratch can save you a few bucks, too.

HOW TO USE THIS COOKBOOK

As with *Maine Home Cooking*, the recipes here appear in topically organized chapters.

Classic Maine Dishes comes first containing some of the old recipes that home cooks used to make everyday fare for growing families, often frugal, and often overlooked these days. They deserve a revival.

Winter Warmers and **Summer Suppers and Summer Lunches** follow. When someone asks me what my favorite thing to eat is, I have to reply that it depends on the season. With a garden where I grow lots of the vegetables I eat. Butternut squash in the fall, apples as we head into winter, asparagus in spring, strawberries in late June, and cucumber sandwiches in July with the first ripe cuke I find, all appeal in turn. Pasta salads in summer, and beany soups in winter.

These two chapters offer up seasonally appropriate dishes, though, of course, if you have a hankering for a braised meat dish in August or a crunchy salad in February, by all means go for it.

If you need a dessert afterwards, turn to the chapter **A Mountain of Desserts** with lots of choices for the sweet tooth.

Good Morning offers up something different for breakfast. We often eat the same breakfast food day after day, and it may be that trying one of these recipes will wait until the weekend when there seems to be more time to experiment. Or perhaps a wrinkle on one of your old favorites will catch your eye and give you a different way to start your day.

You'll find recipes for holiday fare in **Celebrate**. Major and minor holidays appear in order with helpful recipes to match the occasion.

Over the years, Taste Buds collected drinkables to which I added a few of my favorite beverages. Hot and cold, and with spirits and without, the **Have a Drink** chapter isn't exactly a bartender's guide but it suggests a few ways to vary beverages, often with homemade cordials and liqueurs.

Finally, a chapter called **Doing It Yourself** has a collection of recipes for some of the products we buy pre-made but could easily replicate at home at less expense and at our convenience.

Why don't you join me in the kitchen along with many Maine cooks, past and present, where, as the sign on the Maine turnpike in Kittery claimed, we can cook up "the way life should be."

1
CLASSIC MAINE DISHES

Because writing a weekly newspaper column over the years put me in contact with lots of Maine home cooks with long personal and family memories, I collected a grand assemblage of old-fashioned, traditional homemade dishes, some hardly ever made now, and some nearly forgotten.

They come from collections of family recipes, many already published in *Maine Home Cooking*, published in 2012 by Down East Books. The classics in this chapter bubbled up since, often accompanied by charming stories. They still taste good and deserve a place at your table.

REAL MAINE BAKED BEANS

. . .

{ADVICE}

>> *Two pounds of beans produces about a gallon baked. I end up spooning some into quart containers to freeze for another day as home-made fast food. Don't forget the brown bread, the ham or hot dogs, and some pickles.*

If you wish to make vegetarian baked beans, to add flavor add tamari, miso, toasted sesame oil, olive oil or vegetarian Worcestershire sauce to the beans before baking.

Baked beans have sustained Mainers since settlement, even though there were times in the 20th century when eating beans suggested one's family might be cutting the budget a little closely. One old timer told me that the pot of beans was whisked off her family dining table when an aspiring boyfriend came to call, lest he think the family had fallen on hard times.

Mainers like big beans; pea beans are for Boston, and Yellow Eyes are Maine's first choice. Jacobs Cattle, Soldier Beans, Great Northerns, Marafax, and a few other heirloom beans also find favor, though they are harder to find in grocery stores. One reader wrote me that Marafax were always used in the lumber camps, but I had at least one other reader say his grandfather cooked in the camps and "always" used yellow eye. So there you go. Marafax are a personal favorite of mine, and I grow them. The Kennebec Bean Company in North Vassalboro, Maine, carried them twenty years ago under the State of Maine Bean label; I was heartbroken when they stopped selling them.

2 POUNDS OF YELLOW EYE (OR OTHER LARGE DRIED) BEANS

½ POUND SALT PORK

½ CUP MOLASSES

¼ CUP SUGAR

2 TEASPOONS DRY MUSTARD

½ TEASPOON PEPPER

PINCH OF SALT

1 MEDIUM ONION

Soak the beans overnight with enough water to cover generously. Next day, boil the beans until the skins peel back when you blow upon a spoonful. Preheat an oven to 250 (to bake for eight hours) or 300 (to bake for six hours). Put the beans together with the salt pork, molasses, sugar, mustard, salt and pepper, and onion in a bean pot, and add enough water to barely cover the beans. Put the pot into the oven and bake for six to eight hours, checking from time to time and adding water if beans on top look dry. Remove the lid for the last hour or so.

SWAGGON

We need a bean swaggon revival. What a warm and comforting, richly beany, chowder-like dish!

Unbelievably economical, swaggon is nutritious as all-get-out. Legumes like beans and peas, when combined with dairy products and/or grains turn vegetable matter into complete proteins nutritionally comparable to meat. A pot of swaggon will fortify you for anything that hard times and a cold Maine winter can throw at you.

Swaggon Stories

The origin of the name swaggon remains a mystery to me, though I hunted through all my usual etymological sources.

Readers generously provided stories and recipes. Bev Bubar wrote to say that she remembered her grandmother cooking swaggon all day on the back of the woodstove.

Then Alan Badine, writing from way out West, asked about it, too.

Alan's family worked in Maine logging camps. He wrote, "All I can recall is that the main ingredient of the dish was beans, and was wet, but more like a stew than soup, with the bean liquor retained."

Ann Smith in St. Albans and Judi Smith in Hampden sent recipes. Ann says she has made swaggon for fifty years, and that the "not very precise" recipe she uses came down through her husband's family. She suggested a hot biscuit to go with it, and a crisp dill pickle. Judi Smith in Hampden found her recipe in the Herman Senior Citizen Club cookbook from 1982 originally submitted by Delmont Getchell.

Imagine my delight when Jill Holt from Hampden subsequently wrote me that Del Getchell was her uncle, Jill's mom's brother. Jill grew up in Aroostook County and wrote, "I grew up on simple food like [swaggon] ... uncomplicated, delicious and also nutritious. We ate a lot of beans, usually baked, and we never got tired of them. In fact, everyone in my large family still loves beans."

DEL GETCHELL'S SWAGGON

1 TO 2 POUNDS OF DRY BEANS

WATER

¼ TO ½ POUND OF SALT PORK CUBED

1 SMALL ONION CHOPPED

1½ TO 3 CUPS HALF-AND-HALF, EVAPORATED, OR WHOLE MILK

2 TABLESPOONS OF BUTTER

SALT AND PEPPER

Put the beans, pork, and onion in a large Dutch oven or other heavy cook pot. Cover with cold water. Cook over medium heat, covered, stirring every fifteen minutes or so, until the beans soften, adding water to keep the beans covered. When the beans are completely soft and begin to break cup, cut the heat to very low, remove the pot cover, and add the milk and butter. Heat through, add salt and pepper to taste. {Serves 4 to 8}

• • •

Tomato Stew

When Jill Holt sent me her swaggon memories, she went on to recall that her family's evening meal was often what they called Tomato Stew. Simply scalded milk seasoned with salt and pepper to which canned tomatoes, often home-canned, were added, "It was," she wrote, "so tasty served with saltine crackers. Simple food, economical food that satisfied a large growing family."

Like swaggon, it's another exceedingly economical and wholesome supper. As Jill said, "If a family could make just a couple of these simple and cheap meals a week, it could really make a difference in their budgets."

Jill recalled her mom often used home canned tomatoes, evaporated milk, and that she added a bit of baking soda to keep the mixture from curdling. I use a pint of my own home-canned tomatoes from my garden, to which I often add a couple of leaves of basil and a clove of garlic. Round the tomatoes off to the nearest whole can and for the quantities that follow, just get as close to sixteen ounces as you can.

1 12-OUNCE CAN OF EVAPORATED MILK OR 2 CUPS WHOLE MILK

1 CUP OF WATER

1 TEASPOON BAKING SODA

1 PINT OR 2 CUPS OF CANNED STEWED TOMATOES, NOT DRAINED

Put the milk and water into a heavy bottomed pan and set over a medium flame to scald it. When you see bubbles around the edge of the pan, add the baking soda and stir in. Then add the tomatoes and heat through. Don't allow it to boil. Put crackers or toast, buttered if you wish, into the soup bowls and ladle the tomato stew over it. {*Serves 4*}

• • •

Bang Belly

One reader sent along an article authored by a Canadian Maritimes writer, Monique Gibouleau, who learned to make bang-belly from her mother Marie. Marie described bang belly as "a dessert my mother says 'brings you right through the season.' First rhubarb, then strawberries, raspberries, blackberries and finally blueberries became the basis of the summer dessert-of-desserts for the Giboleaus. Her description of a fruit pudding with a drop biscuit, made in a deep casserole dish, puts bang belly in the same class as grunts, slumps, and cobblers.

Another food memory from The County (that is, Aroostook,) came from a reader whose husband grew up with it and hankered for some, specifically blueberry bang belly. A recipe found on the web attributes one Blueberry Bang Belly recipe to a Mrs. Heloise Williston.

This means you can merely stew up the fruit of your choice, especially berries, whatever is in season, and top it with your favorite sweetened biscuit mix and bake it.

Just please don't ask how it got the name Bang Belly, which has been lost in the sands of time.

FILLING:

4 CUPS BLUEBERRIES

1½ CUPS SUGAR (OR LESS IF DESIRED)

3 TABLESPOONS FLOUR

TOPPING:

- 2 CUPS FLOUR
- 1 TEASPOON SALT
- 2 TEASPOONS BAKING POWDER
- ⅔ CUP BUTTER OR SHORTENING
- ½ CUP MILK

Combine the blueberries, sugar, and flour in a saucepan. Cook together until the mixture bubbles. Spread the filling in a greased nine-by-thirteen-inch cake pan. Preheat the oven to 400 degrees. In a bowl, whisk or stir together the flour, salt, and baking powder. Cut in the shortening until the flour looks like coarse corn meal. Add the milk and stir until the dough forms a ball. Flour a board lightly and roll the dough out about a half inch thick or slightly less, sufficient to cover the berries, and lay on top of the blueberry mixture. Bake for twenty to thirty minutes or until the crust is golden brown. Cut in squares and serve from pan.

• • •

LOBSTER ROLLS

{ADVICE}

>> One of the first things I learned from a reader of my column was how to freeze lobster meat. The late Eleanor Campbell of Gouldsboro, and the mom of my island neighbor, the late Connie Leach, told me to just break off the claws, tails, and legs, and freeze the lobster in its shell in a plastic bag. When you thaw the lobster, you can pick it out just as if it was freshly cooked.

The best lobster roll recipe is probably the one you personally prefer; there's no lack of opinions about them among the general populace. I turned to Mildred "Brownie" Schrumpf, whose weekly food column graced the pages of the *Bangor Daily News* for about 43 years and whose recipe you'll find below

When Brownie wrote about lobster for salad or filling for rolls in Memories from Brownie's Kitchen, she recommended cooking enough for boiled lobster one day, then having lobster stew the next, then, finally salad or lobster rolls.

The proper Maine way to serve the lobster filling uses a top split roll with butter-toasted sides. How many rolls you can make with this recipe is really a matter of personal taste. You may be willing to risking a little spillage with a generously stuffed roll, or perhaps you like a more manageable one. Your choice.

- 2 CUPS OF LOBSTER MEAT, CHOPPED LIGHTLY
- JUICE OF HALF A LEMON
- FINELY CHOPPED SHALLOT, OPTIONAL, TO TASTE
- ½ CUP FINELY CHOPPED CELERY

MAYONNAISE TO MIX TO TASTE

SALT AND PEPPER

TOP SPLIT ROLLS WITH FLAT SIDES

Mix the lobster meat with the lemon juice and set aside in the refrigerator. When you are ready to make the rolls, toss the lemon, shallot, celery, and mayonnaise together. Spread the sides of the rolls with butter and grill them until they are golden. Fill each one with the desired amount of lobster filling and serve. Makes about two cups plus a little more of filling.

• • •

POUTINE

As with so many popular dishes, the history of this combination of French fries, cheese curds and gravy is full of competing origin stories, though most seem to point to the mid-1900s in French Canadian restaurants or snack bars where French fries were produced most easily in fryolators. Poutine has found its way into lots of Maine restaurants, even high end ones. And as with so many comfort foods, cheese-rich poutine is high in calories, too. One source declared that the word poutine means mess, and it is a lovely mess, all melty and gravy covered.

A perfectly acceptable version of something akin to deep fried potatoes is possible with oven-roasted potatoes made with plenty of oil, or if you have it, duck or chicken fat.

2 TO 3 TABLESPOONS FAT OR VEGETABLE OIL

2 LARGE OR 4 MEDIUM POTATOES, PEELED AND CUT INTO FRIES

½ PINT OF CHEESE CURDS

1 CUP GRAVY, PREFERABLY PORK

SALT AND PEPPER TO TASTE

Heat the oven to 475 or 500. Melt the fat and oil together in a heavy baking or roasting pan. Distribute the potatoes in the pan, tossing to coat all sides with oil, but making sure there is a single layer. Put them into the oven. Check the potatoes after ten minutes and if they are golden on the pan side flip them over and put them back for another ten minutes. Meanwhile, make

{ADVICE}

« Cut the potatoes thick like steak fries, or in slender sticks like classic French fries. Use a very hot oven, and make sure there is a single layer of potatoes to insure that they will be crisp and golden. At 475 to 500 the potatoes will roast up in fifteen to twenty minutes. If you are very good at paying attention, you could venture 525 or 550 and they will roast in less time.

A fun snack food, cheese curds squeak pleasantly when you bite into them, and are readily found at most grocery stores. Essentially curds are milk curdled and drained from the whey, but not pressed, the product of the first step in making hard cheese. Sometimes flavored with herbs or hot peppers, or sometimes just plain, curds melt readily in the hot potatoes.

the gravy or heat up pre-made gravy. When the potatoes are golden brown, add the curds to them and toss to distribute, then stick them back into the oven to melt the cheese, about three minutes. Remove from the oven and dribble the gravy over the potatoes and cheese and serve. {Serves 2}

• • •

Genuine Mincemeat

Most commercial mincemeat is devoid of meat, with perhaps only a little meat flavoring added. Read the label and you may find you can feed it to a vegetarian.

Here in Maine, however, some still make mincemeat using venison from hunting season, traditionally neck meat because you can just boil it off the bones.

If you lack venison, substitute inexpensive lean beef. Suet (along with lard) has a bad reputation these days but is really a necessary addition for proper flavor. Many prefer to chop the meat and apples in a food processor, while some use an old-fashioned crank grinder. I pull out a wooden chopping bowl and a chopping blade that I've had for years. It takes energy (read calories) to use it, and I like the amount of control I have over how finely the meat, suet, and apples come out.

Sweetening is adjustable. Some recipes call for molasses, plus sweet cider, and sugar in some combination. Personally, I am a cider and brown sugar fan, and I also use brandy. Feel free to increase the proportion of apples to meat if you wish. Spicing is variable, too. Season to taste.

I want to hear a soft squishing noise when I stir the mincemeat, and I add cider until the mixture glistens.

The recipe below that I have used for a few years now is based on three or four older recipes that I have, and it will make enough mincemeat for two pies. Double it or halve it. I usually put mine in a crock and keep it in the unheated wood room between the house and barn. You can keep yours in the fridge or even can it.

1 POUND OF LEAN BEEF OR VENISON

4 TO 6 OUNCES BEEF SUET

2 POUNDS OF APPLES

1 POUND OF CURRANTS

1 POUND OF RAISINS

1½ CUPS OF BROWN SUGAR

¼ CUP BRANDY

1 PINT OF SWEET CIDER

JUICE AND RIND OF A LEMON OR ORANGE

½ TEASPOON FRESHLY GROUND PEPPER

1 TEASPOON OF SALT

2 TABLESPOONS CINNAMON

1 TABLESPOON CLOVES OR ALLSPICE

1 TABLESPOON NUTMEG

Put the beef and suet in water to barely cover it, and cook until the meat is fork tender. Take the meat and suet out, retain the cooking water, and allow the meat to cool until firm enough to handle. Chop finely and put into a large bowl. Peel (if you wish), core and chop the apples. Chop the raisins coarsely. Mix the meat, suet, apples, raisins, and currants together and add the sugar, brandy, cider, orange or lemon, and spices. Mix together and cook over a low heat until the apples are translucent and the raisins and currants have plumped up. Cool and store in the fridge until you are ready to use it. {Yields two quarts}

A Bowl Full of Ingredients

*O*ver the years, I've collected recipes which measure mincemeat ingredients by the bowlful. My Bangor dental hygienist was the first to tell me about her grandmother measuring by the bowlful which alerted me to the practice. The size of the bowl doesn't matter as long as you use the same bowl for each item. Spice is added to taste.

Islesboro's Edna Durkee was famous for her cooking and her mincemeat recipe was measured by the bowl, specifically two bowls of ground meat, five of ground apples, one of ground suet, one bowl of raisins, one of meat cooking juice, two of sugar, half a bowl of molasses, a scant bowl of vinegar, then cloves and nutmeg. "Simmer for hours and hours till apple and suet is done," say the instructions. I'll bet that mincemeat was delicious.

Cheesecake Mincemeat Pie

Back along, a kind reader sent in a recipe labeled "Delish," for Cheesecake Mincemeat Pie, a great way to use mincemeat.

Talk about gilding the lily. A layer of mincemeat in the pie plate, with cream cheese, sugar, and egg poured over, then topped at the last with slightly sweetened sour cream and vanilla, makes for a very tasty wrinkle on old fashioned mincemeat pie.

1 LIGHTLY BAKED PIE SHELL

8 OUNCES SOFTENED CREAM CHEESE

1 EGG

⅓ CUP SUGAR

2 CUPS MINCEMEAT

1 CUP SOUR CREAM

2 TABLESPOONS SUGAR

½ TEASPOON VANILLA

Heat an oven to 375 degrees. Line a nine-inch pie plate with pastry and bake for about 15 minutes, or until light brown and firm. Combine the cream cheese, sugar, and egg in a food processer, or beat it together very well with a mixer, until it is smooth and liquid. Spread the mincemeat in the pie shell, then top with the cream cheese mixture, spreading it evenly over the mincemeat. Bake it for about twenty-five minutes or until it is set but not browned. Whisk together the sour cream, sugar and vanilla, and pour that over the top of the baked pie and return it to the oven for another five minutes. Cool slightly, then chill for six hours (or overnight) before serving. {Makes one nine-inch pie}

The Milk Toast Papers

*A*n old-fashioned and very economical dish, milk toast has been around for centuries. Sometimes called cream toast or brewis, preceded boxed cereal to put milk on.

A good way to use up stale bread or biscuits, it served as a simple supper for a large, hungry family, so when Ellen Askren sent a query from her 89-year-old mom, who remembered *her* mother making large pans full, I collected milk toast memories and recipes from a couple dozen Mainers.

No one has to be sick to relish milk toast, though many, many Down Eastern-ers told me it was what, as Bette Adkins in Corinth wrote, "My mother made for us when we were under the weather." Certainly, milk toast was a common recipe in the invalid cookery sections of cookbooks which hardly any cookbook has today.

Occasionally, as Allison Keef in Hamden and Joanne Macedo in Carmel recalled, the milk toast might be sprinkled with sugar and cinnamon, espe-cially if they were sick. Betsy Bartholomew of Tenants Harbor wrote, "I remem-ber my grandmother making milk toast for us when were feeling poorly. This was in the early '40s. She heated milk (on her wood stove). In a bowl she'd place toast on which she'd sprinkled sugar, then pour the warm milk over the toast."

Persis Wasson of Northeast Harbor wrote to say that she remembered her grandmother making milk toast, but "I never saw her use a recipe." Lots of people said the same thing, though recipes did appear in the *Joy of Cooking* as Jane Johnson of Forest City Township noted. Diane Clough in Bridgewater examined a couple of editions of Fanny Farmer's cookbook and observed that milk toast disappeared from the 7th edition published in 1941. "Milk Toast apparently fell out of favor, perhaps because of increases in personal income," Diane suggested.

Charlene Holyoke of Bangor and Linda Throckmorton in Cutler shared the recipe from the 1944 *Good Housekeeping Cook Book*. Judy Cameron in Dyer Brook reported, "My white sauce recipe comes from *Food, The Yearbook of Agriculture, 1959*, issued by the United States Department of Agriculture.

LeonNa Gilbert, writing from Alabama, shared recipes she found in old cookbooks from the early 1900s. Bruce Hutchins in Montville turned to the 1887 *White House Cook-Book* and Anne Arnold in Millbridge dug "Baked Milk Toast" out of Marion Harland's *Cook Book*, 1906 edition.

Clearly milk toast served as an inexpensive Sunday night supper. Homemade bread like Jill Hoyt of Hamden remembered from her Aroostook childhood toasted on top of the woodstove, ("It made the best toast," she wrote), farm churned butter, and milk from the family cow made milk toast special. Roger Frey, who grew up in Dresden Mills, recalled, "The butter and milk came from a nearby farm with about 8 hand-milked cows. Milk was 25 cents a quart with a lot of cream on top that could be siphoned off for things like whipped cream or coffee. Butter was 50 cents a pound, hand churned by the farmer's wife." Lucille Briggs writing from Glenburn said, "We lived on a farm and had our own butter home made."

Ruth Dugan of Bangor wrote to say, "My mother (bless her heart) was second only to Paula Deen in her love of butter." Sure enough, Ruth's recipe called for butter in the cream sauce, butter on the bread, and then, she wrote, "We topped it with salt and pepper and—are you ready?—a dab more of butter! Yum-yum."

Occasionally hard-boiled chopped eggs were added, as Roger Frey recalled. Jill Hoyt said of her mother, "And sometimes when there was no meat she would make the cream gravy," the same one as for milk toast, "and add sliced, boiled eggs to it and serve it over potatoes. So good!" Persis Wasson said, "Once I remember she (mother) chopped up a few hardboiled eggs in it—but not as a rule."

For most, the milk toast memory was a good one and recalled as delicious, but not everyone loved it. Minnie McCormick wrote, "I know the family ate it a lot on Sunday nights. I didn't care for this but most of the family did." Minnie's mom served it with home-canned fruit on the side. "We picked lots of field strawberries which you can almost never find anymore, wild raspberries and blackberries. She also canned plums, grapes, pears."

Allison Keef recalled cubed toast on warm milk: "As one might expect, the texture was slimy because it was…soaked bread. Today the thought of Milk Toast makes me shudder." My sister Sally Vaster in Somerville emailed me reminding me that our mom never made milk toast. (I do recall mom telling me about milk and crackers—old fashioned cream biscuits—as a Sunday night supper during the Depression and she and dad in their declining years, often had a milk and crackers supper, clearly in the same camp as milk toast.) Sally and I both grew up thinking that maybe milk toast wasn't so good, never even tried it.

I was in for a surprise. Ethel Pochoki from Brooks, called me up and described how to make the cream sauce and biscuits variety of milk toast. She spoke of making the cream sauce milky enough that the biscuits could soak it up a bit. Phyllis Whittier in Dover-Foxcroft wrote describing it as "an easy white sauce," which I make all the time: butter melted, flour stirred in and milk added, and cooked until it thickens. I did have stale baking-powder biscuits on hand; Sharon Reardon, who is firmly in the biscuit and cream sauce camp, had written cautioning, "Do not use biscuit out of a can or yeast bread for substitutes for these recipes. They just won't do."

Persis Wasson had written that her mother's milk toast was never on regular bread. "Always biscuits that were several days old and needing to be used up."

With their advice ringing in my ears, I put it together, added butter, salt and pepper, leaned my back against the warm cook stove and dug in. "Well, well, well," I thought, "I'll be darned. This is *so* good."

Yes, it is a bit starchy, but no worse than a pile of pancakes for breakfast, or a bowl of corn flakes. I can see that it would be just the ticket for someone recovering from gastrointestinal distress. Huddy Peterson in Harrington wrote, "I was telling my granddaughter about this toast. Of course she had never heard of it. I wish I wasn't dieting, because I would love some right now."

• • •

HUDDY'S PLAIN MILK TOAST

Toast the bread. Butter the toast. Heat the milk in a sauce pan on the stove. Pour the milk over it and add salt and pepper.

• • •

SHARON'S MILK TOAST WITH CREAM SAUCE, BISCUIT VERSION

5 HOMEMADE BISCUITS, A DAY OR TWO OLD, CUT INTO HALF-INCH
    THICK SLICES
2 CUPS OF COLD MILK
3 TABLESPOONS OF FLOUR
⅔ OF A STICK OF BUTTER
SALT AND PEPPER TO TASTE

Toast biscuit slices under a broiler in an oven, turning once to brown both sides to a medium brown. Set them aside. Make a plain white sauce in a large saucepan by whisking together cold milk with the flour. Heat over medium high heat, stirring constantly until thickened. Stir in the butter. Reduce the temperature to low just to keep it warm. Next, using boiling water and a slotted spoon, quickly dip toast slices into hot water to moisten, only a second or two. (Too long in the water and the biscuit will fall apart.) Add the moistened toasted biscuits to the thickened milk, pushing them under with a spoon, keeping the toast as whole as possible. Do not stir. Let toast and milk mixture sit ten to fifteen minutes to warm through. Scoop up and serve in soup bowls. {Makes 3 to 4 servings}

Helmi Ranta's Famous Nissua

*E*very Christmas Eve morning, when Ruth Beal grinds cardamom and kneads the Finnish holiday bread called Nissua, a flood of good memories come back. When Ruth, now of Machiasport, was growing up during the 1960s and '70s on Old County Road in Rockand, neighbor Helmi Ranta's door was always open, and her cookie jar was always full.

Helmi's home was a gathering place for many Finnish people who lived in the mid-coast area around Rockland. Ruth, wrote, "Every Tuesday and Friday night the sauna in her back yard was heated up and a steady stream of friends and family waited their turn to enjoy the sauna," playing cribbage and enjoying a table heaped with cookies and cakes.

"She was a wonderful cook," Ruth reported, "but I always looked forward to Christmas, when she made many loaves of Nissua. Ruth's "splattered and tattered," recipe for the bread came from Helmi.

John Root of Owl's Head also enjoyed Helmi's baking. "One of our favorite gifts at Christmastime in the '70s was a twisted loaf if Nissua concocted in Helmi's kitchen." He must have aspired to baking some himself, and asked Helmi for the recipe, which he stashed away. "I have never dared to try making it but that just may change. Thank you for stirring up the memories." He enclosed the recipe written in Helmi's own hand. "I believe," he wrote, "that it would mean more to you than anyone I know."

I was thrilled to hold the piece of pink paper with the handwritten recipe and think about Helmi and her gift of food and friendship for her Rockland neighbors and friends.

Nissua, Finnish Holiday Bread

Nissua, tender, and aromatic with cardamom, is best served fresh and hot with butter on it, though when a couple days old, it makes grand French toast. Ruth Beal said, "It goes stale quite quickly, so that is always the excuse we use to eat it up ASAP!"

The assembly is straight-forward and would be amenable to an electric mixer if you wished to use one. Really truly grind the cardamom at the last minute if you can. Joanne Fuerst of Mt. Desert, who sent a nissua recipe she founds in the *Maine Times* years ago, calculates that fourteen of those papery cardamom pods provides the right amount of seed. I used a heaping teaspoon of seeds which I put through a retired pepper grinder that I have. Fresh cardamom makes all the difference.

Helmi Ranta's recipe and one from Joanne, both called for evaporated milk. If you lack evap, use two cups of light cream.

1 HEAPING CUP SUGAR

1 HEAPING TEASPOON SALT

1 CAN EVAPORATED MILK, SCALDED

2 PACKETS OR 2 TABLESPOONS DRIED YEAST DISSOLVED IN
    ¾ CUP WARM WATER

½ CUP, OR ONE STICK, BUTTER, MELTED THEN COOLED

4 BEATEN EGGS

1 VERY HEAPING TEASPOON GROUND CARDAMOM (FRESHLY
    GROUND IS BEST)

7 CUPS FLOUR PLUS A LITTLE MORE FOR KNEADING

FOR OPTIONAL FROSTING:

1 CUP CONFECTIONS SUGAR

MILK OR CREAM

Put sugar and salt in a large bowl. Pour scalded evaporated milk over, mix, and allow to cool. Stir in the yeast and water mixture. Add the melted butter and mix, and then add the eggs, cardamom, and five cups of flour. Beat the dough 100 strokes or beat in an electric mixer with a dough hook until all the flour is incorporated; it will be quite soft. Add the rest of the flour and knead until elastic. Place in a greased bowl and let rise until doubled in bulk. Punch down and let rise again. Heat the oven to 350 degrees. Divide dough into thirds to make three loaves. Divide each third into three pieces and form rope-like pieces which you braid. Place loaves on greased or parchment-paper-lined baking sheets and let rise again about 20 minutes. Bake at 350 degrees for forty minutes, or until golden brown, and hollow-sounding when tapped. Cool on racks. If you choose to make a frosting, put a cup of confectioners' sugar into a bowl, and add just a very little milk or cream, mixing to make a pourable icing. Dribble the tops of the nissua loaves with frosting.

• • •

VINEGAR PIE

Making vinegar pie sounds like a prank, but you'll be glad to know there is more of every other ingredient in this pie than vinegar. The main question is why make vinegar pie?

Historically, late in spring in northern climes, when old timers had eaten all the pumpkins and apples, and the rhubarb wasn't up yet, pie ingredients might be a little sparse. As long as the kitchen held eggs, sugar, water, and flour or cornstarch, a cook could make pie. Still one needed some flavoring, like lemon juice, or in the absence of juice, extract. Or vinegar.

There are quite a few members of the sugar pie family, sometimes called transparent pies, including raisin, shoofly, chess, and hugely favored lemon meringue. The book *All Maine Cooking* and a recent Maine Rebekah's cookbook provided examples for vinegar pie. This recipe makes a pie identical to lemon meringue pie, the filling's brilliant yellow color coming from the yolks.

Seriously consider sampling the filling when it is cooked to see if it is lemony enough for you, and add more extract if you wish.

You could save this recipe for April's Fools Day, or you could serve it up wordlessly and just smile beatifically when someone says, "What a delicious lemon meringue pie!"

PASTRY SUFFICIENT FOR ONE CRUST, PREFERABLY 8-INCH DIAMETER

1 CUP SUGAR

2 TABLESPOONS CORNSTARCH

1 TABLESPOON PLUS 2 TEASPOONS VINEGAR

2 TEASPOONS LEMON EXTRACT

1 CUP BOILING WATER

2 EGGS, SEPARATED

4 TABLESPOONS MORE SUGAR FOR MERINGUE

Heat the oven to 450 degrees and line an eight-inch pie plate with the pastry, and bake, weighted, for about twelve to fifteen minutes. Remove from the oven and set aside. Reduce the oven temperature to 350 degrees. Mix the sugar, cornstarch, vinegar, and extract in a small heavy saucepan, and stirring, add the hot water. Cook over a medium heat until it comes to a boil, and cook, stirring gently until it's thick and translucent. Take it off the heat. Separate the eggs, setting the whites aside for a meringue. Stir the yolks and add them to the hot sugar and cornstarch mixture, stirring to combine them. Set aside. Beat the whites until they are nearly stiff; then gradually add four tablespoons of sugar, one tablespoon at a time. Pour the filling into the pie shell and top it with the meringue. Bake for ten to fifteen minutes until the meringue has turned golden. {Makes one pie}

• • •

Indian Pudding

As far as I can tell, making Indian pudding is really about evaporating liquid out of milk. The oldest recipes from New England typically call for one quart of milk, seven large spoons full of cornmeal, and molasses to sweeten. Bake and bake and bake until it looks curdled, and then eat it. Add ice cream or a dribble of cream or whipped cream.

It's a pity this stuff seldom shows up in restaurants anymore, but I think most pastry chefs eschew it because, at best, it looks awfully dumpy in a bowl. You can still buy it canned, but you have to look for it in specialty stores or in the Maine-made section of grocery stores.

If you are an Indian pudding novice, you might wonder at the instructions to "pour over" the cold milk at the end of the assembly process. Of course, you can't actually pour milk over without it mixing in a little. Basically, it means to add milk slowly enough not to agitate the whole mess. You will use a whole quart of milk, and I recommend whole milk, not two or one percent. You need some solids in this recipe.

2 CUPS OF MILK

¼ CUP OF CORNMEAL

¼ CUP COLD MILK

½ CUP MOLASSES

¼ CUP BROWN SUGAR

A PINCH OF SALT

1 TEASPOON CINNAMON

1 TEASPOON GINGER

2 TABLESPOONS BUTTER

1¾ CUP MILK

Heat the oven to 250 degrees. Grease a nine-by-thirteen glass baking dish. Scald two cups of milk in a heavy pan by heating it until you see bubbles around the edge of the pan. Mix the cornmeal and a quarter cup of cold milk together and pour into the hot milk. Cook together, stirring frequently, until it thickens slightly. Add the molasses, sugar, salt and spices, and butter, which will melt, and stir until it is well-mixed. Pour into the baking dish. Gently add the remaining cup and three quarters of cold milk. Bake for three hours. Let it stand a while before serving. {*Makes 6 to 8 servings*}

Indian Pudding and Native Americans

*I*ndian pudding was Colonial America's answer to milk-based grain puddings made in England in the early 1700s. Since corn—maize—which we learned about from the Native Americans, was the primary ground meal in early New England, we simply substituted it for wheat meal, sweetening it with molasses instead of sugar.

Indian pudding got its name from the colonists' habit of referring to maize as "Indian" since English colonists used their word "corn" to refer to wheat. When they said "Indian corn" they were actually saying "the Indians' grain." We didn't learn to make the pudding from the Native Americans because before colonial settlement, they did not keep milk cows so they wouldn't have made this pudding, nor did they import cane sugar or molasses made from it.

Lumberjacks and Crybabies

What do these two have in common? Both are cookies, and pretty similar ones, too. The biggest distinction is oatmeal in the lumberjack recipes and the fact that the recipe can produce one hundred of them. The Crybabies use coffee, or sometimes hot water, as the liquid while the Lumberjacks rely on milk. If you enjoy molasses cookies, either of these recipes will satisfy your hankering..

. . .

Lumberjack Cookies

This astonishing recipe hearkens back to lumber camp days, and yields a dough that the camp cook—or you—can bake up four different ways.

While the recipe below features a dropped-style cookie for baking, variations of the recipe spoke of a deep-fried version, a skillet baked version (like a pancake), and a rolled, cut, and baked version.

I tend to prefer the dropped version because they call for a little less flour, which means they have more flavor. Goodness knows they are easier to make, requiring so little handling.

If you decide to roll and cut, just sift in a little more flour after you mix them all together until the dough is soft but you can handle it. Roll out about a quarter of an inch thick and cut to size. They bake in ten to twelve minutes, or until they are firm.

This recipe makes a lot of cookies. You could make even more by cutting two-inch diameter cookies instead of three-inch ones, or fewer cookies by cutting or dropping really big ones.

Hand these out to your favorite lumberjack or the grandkids, stick them in a lunch bag, dunk them in coffee or tea, or do as Mary Pelkey does and take them to a family reunion.

1 CUP LARD
1 CUP BUTTER

2 CUPS SUGAR

6 CUPS FLOUR

2 TEASPOONS SALT

2 TEASPOONS BAKING SODA

3 TEASPOONS BAKING POWDER

1 TEASPOON CREAM OF TARTAR

½ TEASPOON NUTMEG

½ TEASPOON CLOVES

½ TEASPOON GINGER

½ TEASPOON CINNAMON

3 CUPS RAISINS

2 CUPS OATMEAL

1 CUP MOLASSES

1 CUP MILK

4 EGGS

2 TABLESPOONS VANILLA

½ SMALL ONION (OPTIONAL)

¼ CUP MOLASSES, OR TO TASTE

2 TABLESPOONS MUSTARD SALT AND PEPPER, TO TASTE

Heat the oven to 350 degrees. Grease cookie sheets very well, or line them with parchment paper. Melt the lard and butter together. Meanwhile, sift together into a large bowl all the dry ingredients except the oatmeal and raisins. Add the oatmeal and raisins and combine with the dry ingredients. Whisk together the melted lard and butter and milk, molasses, eggs and vanilla. Add the liquids to the dry ingredients and mix until all the dry ingredients are incorporated. This makes a soft dough. Drop by teaspoonfuls on the cookie sheet. Bake for twelve to fifteen minutes, until they are puffed slightly and feel firm. Cool on a rack.

• • •

CRYBABIES

I had a fine time figuring out what distinguished Crybabies from various other molasses cookies. It is a close call, but the assemblage of recipes I had in hand seemed to show a consistent use of melted shortening and often hot coffee, though coffee also appears in molasses cookies. They are lightly spiced, usually with ginger and cinnamon, though Cora's recipe called also for cloves and allspice.

Minnie's, Cora's, and one of Betty's recipes showed a striking resemblance to one another, minus the chocolate chips in Minnie's. What follows is a mash-up of the three. All the recipes called for "shortening" and I used butter. Because I enjoy spice, I doubled up on it, not reflected in the recipe below. You'll want to add spice to your taste. I made fairly daintily-sized cookies,

Crybabies Backstory

*Y*ou don't have to be a whiney little kid to be comforted by these pillowy soft, lightly spiced molasses cookie. Personally, I'd whine for hours until someone gave me one of these cookies. Save them to pass out to crying kiddos in case of skinned knees or some similar calamity.

Retired home economics teacher Alice Knight of Rockland wrote that John Gould's 1975 *Maine Lingo* identified the cookie as a soft sugar cookie with a filling of mincemeat, raisins, or jam, though Alice applied the name to any large soft cookie she took to bake sales.

Minnie McCormick supplied a recipe from *Cooking With a Maine Accent*, published by the Gorham Woman's Club in 1992 in honor of the Maine General Federation of Women's Clubs Cookie Leclair of the Hinckley Kennebecside Club, no longer in existence. Minnie's recipe called for chocolate chips, and Minnie wrote, "I hadn't thought of chocolate chips with molasses."

Well, I wouldn't have thought of it, either. In fact, I think it is a lousy idea. People put chocolate chips in too many things; it's a wonder they aren't part of meat loaf these days.

Then, from East Millinocket, Cora Cox sent a recipe, too, her grandmother's, which came to Cora by way of her Aunt Martha Elliot. "Grammie used to have a restaurant in East Millinocket," wrote Cora, "and was well-known for her baking."

Fellow food writer Betty Heald whose column, "Baking with Betty" appears in the Camden and Belfast papers, sent two Crybaby recipes plus, for comparison, two soft molasses cookie recipes.

and the recipe yielded over a hundred of them. The recipe is easily halved, or you can make bigger cookies.

4½ CUPS FLOUR

2 TEASPOON CINNAMON

2 TEASPOON GINGER

½ TEASPOON CLOVES, OPTIONAL

½ TEASPOON ALLSPICE, OPTIONAL

2 TEASPOONS BAKING SODA

1 TEASPOON SALT

1 CUP SUGAR

1 CUP MOLASSES

1 CUP MELTED BUTTER OR SHORTENING

2 EGGS

1 TEASPOON VANILLA

1 CUP OF HOT COFFEE

1 CUP RAISINS

1 CUP WALNUTS CHOPPED, OPTIONAL

Double Scrub Stories

*M*achias' Ruth Thurston inquired a few years ago if anyone had ever heard of a hot water chocolate cake going by the name Double Scrub. A reader sent along a wonderful story about a recipe she has named Double Scrub that came from a church cookbook dated 1937 which she inherited from her grandmother. It was a favorite in her family, and she recounted good memories of her grandmother's wood cook stove in the kitchen where she learned to make molasses cookies and pie crust using lard.

And then, Marlene Kamas in Monroe recognized the recipe as the same as her "Annette's Chocolate Cake," another family favorite. She sprinkles the top of it with powdered sugar and doesn't bother frosting it.

Likely, Double Scrub is another name for the quirky and delicious hot water chocolate cake.

Heat the oven to 375. Grease baking sheets or line with parchment paper. Sift together the flour, spices, baking soda, and salt. Beat together the sugar, molasses, and shortening, and then add the eggs and vanilla, and beat well. Stir in the flour mixture until the flour is entirely incorporated. Add the hot coffee and mix to make a smooth batter. Fold in raisins and nuts, if desired. Drop spoonfuls on the baking sheets allowing room for spreading. Bake for ten to twelve minutes. Cool before storing in an airtight container.

. . .

Hot Water Chocolate Cake

My island neighbor and friend Pat Mitchell brings this cake to potlucks and our monthly Sewing Circle birthday observances. She kindly shared the recipe.

Pat describes this as a "dump cake," which means you can more or less dump the ingredients together in usual cake fashion, with virtually no fuss. It goes quickly.

⅓ CUP VEGETABLE OIL

1 CUP SUGAR

1 EGG

1 TEASPOON VANILLA

2 OUNCES BAKING CHOCOLATE, MELTED

1½ CUP FLOUR

1 TEASPOON BAKING SODA

¼ TEASPOON SALT

1 CUP BOILING WATER

Heat the oven to 350 degrees and grease an eight-inch round pan. Beat together the oil and sugar, then beat in the egg. Add the melted chocolate and vanilla and beat enough to mix well. Sift together the flour, baking soda and salt. Add the flour mixture and water alternately to the oil, sugar, egg and chocolate batter, beating slowly and ending with the water. Pour into the cake pan and bake for thirty minutes or until a tester inserted comes out clean. Frost if desired, or serve with whipped cream. {Makes 1 eight-inch cake}

{ADVICE}

« The surprise here is the hot water. When you add the water called for, the batter is alarmingly thin, looking more like something to drink than to bake. In fact, I was concerned enough that I called Pat up to check on it. She said, "This isn't like other cake batters," so I proceeded.

Two things I tweaked were to replace a bit of the flour with cocoa just to amp up the chocolate a bit. And I added a teaspoon of instant espresso coffee powder to the hot water because I read somewhere that even if you can't taste the coffee, it enhances the chocolate flavor overall.

Pat often doubles the recipe to make enough for a layer cake. I decided I would double the recipe, too, and bake mine in a tube pan, which Pat said she hasn't yet tried to do. It came out beautifully. In the recipe below, I provide the ingredients for the basic single layer cake that Pat gave me. If you double it, and bake it in two pans, you'll need thirty minutes' baking time. If you choose a tube pan, you need closer to fifty minutes for baking. Just insert your tester to make sure it comes out clean and look for the cake pulling away from the sides of the pan.

2

Winter Warmers

Chances are, if you live in Maine, you spend more months cooking up warm meals than producing cooling fare. Still, a mid-October chill makes chili taste good and we still welcome a hot soup in April.

⇛ SOUP ⇚

. . .

Danish Soup

Ethel Pochocki's cookbook *Holy Housewifery* offered seventeen soup recipes. However, she explained, "In case you are still nervous about attempting anything undirected," she included soup recipes with quantities and instructions. But first she wrote, "Now is the time to clean out the refrigerator."

I am a girl after Ethel's heart; I never actually follow a recipe for soup, so her Danish Soup caught my eye because it matched the local supply: a ham bone with a little meat still attached, potatoes, carrots, celery, cabbage. Of *course*, I didn't follow it to the letter. I thought my soup needed a little more meat, so added chourizo I'd made with venison. I left out the flour. Instead of cream, I tossed in a small collection I had of parmesan cheese rinds. Ethel would have approved.

A HAM BONE WITH SOME MEAT ON IT

2 POTATOES

BUNCH OF GREEN ONIONS WITH THE TOPS ON

3 STALKS OF CELERY WITH TOPS

2 CUPS CHOPPED GREEN CABBAGE

2 CARROTS

¼ CUP CHOPPED PARSLEY

3 TABLESPOONS FLOUR

1 CUP CREAM

SALT AND PEPPER TO TASTE

YOUR CHOICE OF HERBS OR SEASONINGS

Boil the ham bone in about two quarts of water until the meat falls from it, at least one hour. Remove bone. Chop the vegetables, but not too finely, and add to the ham broth. Cook until they are tender, about forty minutes. Pour a little cold water into the flour whisking until it is a smooth paste; then add it to the soup. Bring the soup to a boil. Add the cream and seasonings of your choice. Serve right away or reheat later for serving.

Remembering Ethel Pochocki

Ethel Pochocki of Brooks corresponded faithfully with Taste Buds early on, sending along good recipes and ideas; we even talked on the phone, with the kind of friendly connection I've been blessed with over the years with lots of readers. So when word came that Ethel had passed away, I was genuinely sad. Then another reader and a neighbor of Ethel's sent me *Holy Housewifery Cookbook*, described as "The hilarious collection of 569 recipes with a text designed to make housewives giggle while they cook. A joy to read and use," authored in 1968 by Ethel Marbach Pochocki.

Ethel *was* genuinely funny. In the head notes for a sausage dish, she wrote, "Very hearty and heartburny. When you smell this cooking, you feel you should be out chopping wood so you could come in and deserve it. I'd *rather* be out chopping wood than cooking with it, but that is the way the kielbasa bounces."

The mother of eight, a gardener, cook, and author, Ethel graduated from Katherine Gibbs School in New York, but wrote in her author bio, "You don't know how tempted I am to write, 'graduated from Meadowlark Reformatory for Delinquent Dieticians or *something* better than 'former secretary for book, cloth manufacturers.'"

What a lively spirit.

· · ·

Tomato Soup

Tomato soup is one of our ultimate comfort foods, especially served with a grilled cheese sandwich. You can make it easily, especially if you adopt the philosophy that, "If it is red and used to be a tomato, it is fair game for soup."

1 TO 2 TABLESPOONS OLIVE OR VEGETABLE OIL

1 MEDIUM ONION, CHOPPED, OPTIONAL

1 RIB OF CELERY, CHOPPED, OPTIONAL

2 CLOVES GARLIC, OPTIONAL

1 QUART PLUS OR MINUS PREPARED TOMATO SAUCE, PASTA SAUCE, OR STEWED, DICED TOMATOES

2 TO 3 CUPS BEEF BOUILLON

2 TO 3 TEASPOONS OREGANO

2 TO 3 TEASPOONS BASIL

1 TO 2 TEASPOONS MARJORAM

PINCH OF RED PEPPER FLAKES, OPTIONAL, TO TASTE

SALT AND PEPPER TO TASTE

Put the olive oil in a soup pot, and add the onion and celery, sauté for five minutes or until the vegetables are just tender. Add the garlic and sauté a minute more. Add bouillon and tomatoes and/or sauce and simmer together for twenty minutes. Add herbs and taste, adjusting flavor with salt and pepper, additional herbs if wished. Let simmer over a very low temperature for another twenty minutes. {*Serves 4 to 5*}

SALAD

. . .

WARM GRAIN SALAD

Little grains of barley, farro, wheat, or even rye, boiled until tender but still chewy, accompanied by a little dried fruit, onion, cheese, nuts, bacon, and snappy dressing makes a good warm or room temperature salad alongside a roast or atop lettuce as a stand-alone dish. Wholesome as all get out, too.

WARM FARRO BARLEY SAVORY SALAD

1 CUP EACH OF BOILED FARRO AND BARLEY, OR TWO CUPS

  OF ONE GRAIN

1 MEDIUM ONION, RED OR MILD WHITE, FINELY CHOPPED

½ CUP DRIED CRANBERRIES COARSELY CHOPPED

¼ CUP DRIED CURRANTS

4 TO 5 SCALLIONS, SLICED

⅓ CUP SALTED AND SMOKED ALMONDS, COARSELY CHOPPED

½ CUP GRATED PARMESAN CHEESE

2 TABLESPOONS BALSAMIC VINEGAR

2 TABLESPOONS OLIVE OIL

2 TEASPOONS DIJON-STYLE MUSTARD

½ TEASPOON SALT

¼ TEASPOON PEPPER

4 SLICES OF BACON, FRIED AND CHOPPED

Put the cooked grains into a large bowl and add the onions, cranberries, currants, almonds, and parmesan cheese. In a separate container, whisk together the vinegar, oil, and mustard, and add to the bowl of grain, stirring to distribute the dressing evenly. Let stand at room temperature for a few hours for flavors to meld. Serve at room temperature and warm gently before serving in a low oven or in the microwave. Garnish with the chopped bacon for serving. {Serves 4 to 6}

• • •

Shaved Butternut Squash Salad

Raw butternut squash? Really? I know: what a surprise. Think about how we use carrots, shredded in slaws, or added to a green salad, or shredded or shaved as a stand-alone salad. Of course, eaten raw, more of squash's nutrients stay intact

Inspired by Melissa Clark's advice (in the *New York Times*), use a vegetable peeler to shave squash curls off into a bowl, sprinkle with a little lemon juice, a little olive oil, a shake of salt and some sugar, and a little black pepper. In about twenty minutes, it softens up nicely. if a simple vinaigrette salad dressing is what you have, then by all means use that sparingly at first. You want to soften the squash, not drown it.

Consider shredding squash on a grater with carrots to make a cheerful orange-colored salad, or mixing shredded squashed into cabbage for a slaw variation.

½ TO 1 POUND OF BUTTERNUT SQUASH

½ LEMON, JUICE AND ZEST

2 TABLESPOONS OF OLIVE OIL

½ TEASPOON OF SUGAR

SALT AND PEPPER

2 OR 3 SCALLIONS, CHOPPED

RAISINS OR DRIED CRANBERRIES (OPTIONAL)

SUNFLOWER OR PUMPKIN SEEDS (OPTIONAL)

Peel the butternut, and cut it into easy-to-hold chunks. Shave the squash into a bowl. Sprinkle with lemon juice, zest, oil, sugar and salt and pepper to taste. Let sit for 10 to 20 minutes, sample to see if it has tenderized a little, allow more time as needed. Add in scallions and optional ingredients. Toss and serve.

VEGETABLE SIDE DISHES

. . .

CAULIFLOWER STEAK

Good old cauliflower. Low carbohydrate, low fat, low everything except fiber, potassium, and Vitamin C. Only 146 calories in one medium head. What a nice vegetable.

Cut a couple of slabs out of the middle using the core to hold it together. Each slab looks like a tree, very pretty. You can cut up the rest of the cauliflower into florets to steam; or mash and season them, to make a puree on which to float the steaks.

    1 1½-POUND HEAD OF CAULIFLOWER
    ½ CUP MILK
    2 TABLESPOONS VEGETABLE OIL
    YOUR CHOICE OF PAPRIKA, CUMIN, CORIANDER, CHILI
    SALT AND FRESHLY GROUND PEPPER
    BUTTER

Cut two one-half to three-quarter inch slabs out of the center of a head of cauliflower. Cut the remaining cauliflower into florets and put the florets into a saucepan with the milk plus a little water, and bring to a boil. Reduce the heat and simmer the florets until they are tender. Drain, set aside, and reserve the cooking liquid. Put the florets in a food processor (or use a masher), add a little of the reserved cooking liquid and puree until smooth, adding more liquid to taste. Season puree with salt and pepper, and butter. Set it aside. Heat the oil over medium heat in a heavy frying pan or skillet, sprinkle the oil lightly with the spices, and lay the steaks on the pan. Cook until the steaks brown lightly and are fork tender, turning once. Reheat the puree and spread on a dinner plate and lay the steaks on top to serve. *{Serves 2}*

. . .

Baked Stuffed Acorn Squash

If it is hollow, stuff it. Stuffing acorn squash or any others like Delicatas, Dumplings, or even a small pumpkin, turns the vegetable into a main dish. Seasoned bread crumb stuffing works, as do rice, orzo, couscous, and bulgur. You can also merely stuff it with cooked sausage or hamburger, or a pile of finely chopped, sautéed vegetables.

½ AN ACORN SQUASH PER PERSON (IF FOR A MAIN DISH)
OLIVE OIL
ONION OR LEEKS, FINELY CHOPPED
CELERY OR PARSLEY, FINELY CHOPPED
SAUSAGE OR BACON, FRIED AND CHOPPED UP
DRY BREADCRUMBS, OR RICE OR SMALL PASTA
     COOKED BROTH
HERBS TO TASTE: MARJORAM, THYME, SAGE
SALT AND PEPPER

Heat the oven to 350 degrees Cut the squash in half and scoop out the seeds. Oil a baking pan and place the squash cut side down and bake for twenty to thirty minutes or until it feels soft and a fork can pierce the flesh. Dribble a little oil into a sauté pan and add the onions or leeks, the celery or parsley, and lightly cook for about three minutes. Add the sausage or bacon bits to the vegetables and mix. Sprinkle in the bread crumbs, or grains, and mix, adding just enough broth or water to moisten the stuffing. Season to taste with herbs and salt and pepper. Pile the stuffing into the squash and bake until the top has browned and is crisp, about ten to fifteen minutes.

HIMMEL UND ERDE: COMFORTING DISH FROM HEAVEN AND EARTH

Unbelievably easy to make, Nancy Crooker of Belfast contributed the recipe for this comforting traditional German dish, perfect for winter eating.

Lots of Himmel—heaven—and Erde—earth—recipes call for equal parts of apple and potatoes. The apples represent heaven because they grow on heavenward reaching trees, and potatoes come from the earth. When Nancy makes it, she doubles down on the earth part by adding mashed turnips, a kind of Himmel und Erde und Erde.

Clearly, leftover mashed potatoes and some jarred applesauce are an obvious combination to make this dish in a hurry.

Caramelized onions customarily adorn the top of the combination which makes a great side dish for sausage like bratwurst and, for many Germans, blood sausage.

1 POUND OF POTATOES

2 TABLESPOONS BUTTER

POTATO COOKING WATER

SALT AND PEPPER

1 POUND TART APPLES

WATER

1 LARGE ONION, SLICED

3 TABLESPOONS BUTTER

Peel and boil the potatoes, and when they are done, drain them, reserving some of the cooking water. Mash them with two tablespoons of butter and just enough cooking water to make them smooth. Add salt and pepper to taste and set aside. Core the apples and cut into chunks. Add a couple tablespoons of water and cook over a medium heat until the apples soften. Stir them vigorously to mash them enough to add to the dish. Mix the potatoes and applesauce together. In a heavy pan, melt the three tablespoons of butter and add the sliced onions. Cook over a medium heat, fifteen to twenty minutes, stirring frequently, and adding a little more butter if they begin to dry out, until the onions turn a golden color. Remove from the heat. Serve the applesauce and potato mixture with the onions on top. {*Serves 4*}

. . .

Beet and Squash Latkes

2 MEDIUM BEETS

1 PIECE OF WINTER SQUASH, OR SWEET POTATO THE SIZE OF
 ONE OF THE BEETS

1 QUARTER OF AN APPLE

1 EGG, LIGHTLY BEATEN

¼ TEASPOON THYME, OR TO TASTE

OLIVE OR VEGETABLE OIL

Peel the beets and grate them and the squash or sweet potato. Grate the apple. Put beets, squash, and apple into a bowl and add the egg and thyme. Mix very well. Heat a pan over medium high and add a bit of olive oil. Drop spoonfuls of the vegetable mixture on the pan and flatten with the back of the spoon. Cook until the latkes are golden brown on one side and then flip over to brown the other side. Drain on a paper towel and keep them warm in the oven on low heat while you cook the rest of the latkes. Serve warm with a bit of sour cream, sprinkle of parmesan, or a dribble of vinaigrette. {*Makes 6 to 8 latkes*}

. . .

Cracked Coriander Potatoes

I observed small potatoes smashed and seasoned with coriander in Cyprus when I visited there a number of years ago. A very mild seasoning, coriander is the seed of the plant that produces cilantro leaves.

The potatoes end up being partly steamed and partly fried, quickly done on the stove top. Use small ones, often sold as small roasting potatoes. Slightly waxy potatoes are better than floury sorts; small reds and little Yukon Golds work very nicely.

3 OR 4 SMALL POTATOES PER PERSON

OLIVE OIL

1 TABLESPOON OF WHOLE, CRUSHED CORIANDER SEEDS
OR 2 TEASPOONS OF GROUND CORIANDER, TO TASTE.
SALT AND PEPPER.

Prepare the potatoes by tapping them firmly with the side of a rolling pin until they crack, but do not break into pieces. Heat a heavy pan over a medium heat, dribble a bit of olive oil on it, sprinkle in the seeds, add the potatoes in a single layer. Put a lid on the pan. Check after fifteen minutes, or until the potatoes have a golden crust on the bottom. Turn the potatoes over and repeat. Thirty minutes should be sufficient. Add salt and pepper to taste and serve.

MAIN DISHES

· · ·

Brussels Sprouts and Smoked Sausage

Thanks to the robust flavor of Brussels sprouts and the satisfying smokiness of a sausage like kielbasa, this recipe that came from Mark and Lauren Lewis in Rockland makes a fine, warm, main dish salad. Sliced red onion, a handful of toasted walnuts, and dried cranberries plus sweet and sour dressing reminiscent of the one used for a popular broccoli salad that calls for bacon and raisins. There are two potential dressings below that you can use with the Brussels sprouts and kielbasa. If you mix the dressing separately from the salad, you can use as much or little as you need, and if any is left, use the rest on another salad on a different day.

1½ POUNDS BRUSSELS SPROUTS
1 WHOLE SMOKED SAUSAGE, APPROXIMATELY 14 OUNCES
1 MEDIUM RED ONION
½ CUP WALNUT PIECES, LIGHTLY TOASTED
½ CUP DRIED CRANBERRIES
SALAD

Slice the brussels sprouts thinly or shred on a mandoline into a good-sized bowl. Slice the sausage crosswise into disks about a half inch thick and brown them in a frying pan and add them to the sliced sprouts. Slice the red onion thinly and add. Add the walnuts and cranberries and toss the salad together. Add the dressing of your choice and let stand for fifteen minutes before serving. *{Serves 4 to 8}*

Vinaigrette with Honey:

1 TABLESPOON DIJON-STYLE MUSTARD

¼ CUP RED WINE VINEGAR

1 TABLESPOON HONEY

½ CUP OLIVE OIL

SALT AND PEPPER TO TASTE

Put all ingredients into a bowl or jar with a tight lid. Whisk together or shake jar until dressing is entirely mixed. Sample and adjust salt and pepper to taste and add more honey if desired. *{Makes one scant cup of dressing}*

Sweet and Sour Dressing:

1 CUP MAYONNAISE

¼ CUP HONEY

¼ CUP BROWN SUGAR

2 TABLESPOONS VINEGAR, CIDER, RICE OR RED WINE

SALT AND PEPPER TO TASTE

{Makes about ¾ cup of dressing}

• • •

Taco Pie

Linda Acorn of Islesboro inspired my curiosity about taco pie. She and her husband Bob are fond of it, so I thought it was worth a try. In some ways, taco pie is an upside-down tamale pie. Where tamale pie calls for cornbread on top of the filling, the recipe below calls for a cornbread mixture on the bottom of the baking dish; if you are short on time, however, you can use crushed tortilla chips instead, with the meat and bean mixture on top.

1 TABLESPOON VEGETABLE OIL

1 CLOVE GARLIC, FINELY CHOPPED

1 SMALL ONION, FINELY CHOPPED

1 POUND GROUND BEEF OR VENISON

2 TABLESPOONS TACO SEASONING MIX

½ CUP STEWED TOMATOES OR TOMATO SAUCE

½ CUP BLACK OR KIDNEY BEANS, OPTIONAL

½ CUP FLOUR

½ CUP CORNMEAL

1 TEASPOON BAKING POWDER

1 TABLESPOON MELTED BUTTER OR VEGETABLE OIL

½ CUP MILK

1 EGG

½ CUP GRATED CHEDDAR OR MONTEREY JACK CHEESE, OR TO TASTE.

Heat the oven to 400 degrees. Grease an eight or nine inch baking dish or skillet. Put the oil into a frying pan over a medium heat and cook the garlic and onion until softened, about three minutes; then add the meat and cook until done. Add the taco seasoning and mix well; then add the tomato sauce or stewed tomatoes and optional beans. Reduce the temperature and simmer ingredients together. Mix the flour, cornmeal, and baking powder in a separate bowl. Whisk together the butter or vegetable oil, egg, and milk and add to the dry ingredients. Mix gently just until it makes a soft dough, using more milk if necessary. Spread the cornmeal mixture in the greased baking dish or skillet. Distribute the seasoned meat over the cornbread mixture and top with grated cheese. Bake at 400 for about twenty minutes until a tester inserted comes out clean. {*Serves 4*}

• • •

Spicy Asian-Style Peanut Sauce

Toss this super simple peanut sauce with spaghetti, fettuccine, buckwheat, or ramen noodles for a very simple supper. Use it with a bland protein like chicken, tofu; or shrimp; steamed broccoli or cauliflower, and serve on rice.

¼ CUP HOT WATER

¼ CUP SMOOTH UNPROCESSED PEANUT BUTTER

¼ CUP TAMARI OR SOY SAUCE

2 TABLESPOONS TOASTED SESAME OIL

¼ CUP RICE VINEGAR

¼ CUP FIRMLY PACKED LIGHT BROWN SUGAR

¼ TEASPOON CAYENNE, OR LESS, TO TASTE

2 TEASPOONS FRESH GINGER ROOT, GRATED

1 CLOVE OF GARLIC

Whisk together in a saucepan water, peanut butter, soy or tamari, sesame oil, and vinegar over a low heat until smooth Add sugar, cayenne, ginger, and garlic and heat through.

• • •

KERENE'S CURRIED CHICKEN

While it served dinner to its guests, the Dark Harbor House Inn on Islesboro never put Kerene Spence's wonderful Jamaican-style curried chicken on the menu. She prepared it only for the owner's visiting family members and staff because her traditional version called for keeping the bones in the small chunks of chicken that she tossed together with Jamaican-style curry spices. Jamaicans, Kerene explained, popped a whole chunk into their mouths, chewed the meat off, and sometimes even crunched up the smaller, softer bones and swallowed them!

The curried chicken meat was wonderful, fragrant with allspice, nutmeg, and paprika that she added to her usual curry powder ingredients of turmeric, cumin, coriander, mustard powder, and ginger.

Make sure you use leg and thigh meat as well as breast meat, boneless if you wish. Just remember bones add a great deal of flavor. You can remove them in the kitchen before serving.

You can cook this in a slow oven for a couple of hours, or use a slow-cooker, or Instant-pot.

JAMAICAN-STYLE CURRIED CHICKEN SEASONING

CURRY POWDER

1½ TABLESPOONS TURMERIC

2 TEASPOONS CUMIN

2 TEASPOONS GROUND CORIANDER

1 TEASPOON GINGER

1 TEASPOON BLACK PEPPER

½ TEASPOON MUSTARD POWDER

½ TEASPOON ALLSPICE

¼ TEASPOON NUTMEG

¼ TEASPOON CAYENNE (OPTIONAL)

¼ TEASPOON PAPRIKA

Put into a bowl and whisk together. Set aside.

CURRIED CHICKEN:

VEGETABLE OIL

1 BONE-IN CHICKEN, QUARTERED, THEN CHOPPED INTO BITE-SIZED PIECES

1 LARGE ONION, CHOPPED

2 CLOVES GARLIC, MINCED

½ GREEN PEPPER, CHOPPED

½ RED PEPPER CHOPPED

CURRY POWDER

2 OR 3 SMALL PLUM TOMATOES, CHOPPED

JUICE OF ONE LIME

1 CUP CHICKEN BROTH

SALT AND PEPPER

PARSLEY OR CILANTRO, OPTIONAL

Heat the oven to 300 degrees. Cover the bottom of a heavy pot with oil and add the chicken pieces to brown a little on both sides. Remove to large bowl. Put the onion, garlic, and peppers in the pot and cook until the vegetables are just softened, and distribute them and the chopped tomatoes over the chicken. Sprinkle the curry powder over the chicken and vegetables. Add the lime juice and broth and toss together. Put the chicken and vegetable mix into a nine-by-thirteen baking dish. Cover the baking dish with a lid or cover with foil. Bake for 2 hours, then remove the lid and bake for a half hour to reduce the liquid. Remove from the oven. If desired, remove the bones. If desired, reduce the liquid further in a pan or thicken slightly with flour or cornstarch and pour back over the meat and vegetables. Sample and add salt and pepper to taste. Garnish with chopped parsley or cilantro. {Serves 4 to 6}

Kerene Spence

Three decades ago, Jamaican islander Kerene Spence cooked for Dark Harbor House Bed and Breakfast Inn on Islesboro. Kerene worked as a cook in Jamaica for the inn's owner, Matt Skinner, and worked in Maine for the summer.

I had the great good luck to work alongside her for a couple of summers, and I learned a great deal. She had marvelous capacity for turning a rib of celery into delicate dice using only a paring knife. She pounded chicken breasts flat using only a wine bottle. When she cooked meat, she made an informal dry rub by deftly adding spices by eye. All her recipes were stored between her ears.

Except for wonderful bread pudding, she didn't make desserts; that was my job.

I lost track of Kerene when the bed and breakfast inn was sold, over twenty-five years ago now, and she stopped coming here to work summers, staying in Jamaica full time. Eating the curried chicken, though, was a little like a visit with my old friend.

• • •

Sharon's Deluxe Meatloaf

Not all meatloafs are made equally. Sharon Frost in Calais sent this recipe along, commenting that it was the best thing for family gatherings. She wrote, "My mother made this many times for Legion suppers, etc. Good!"

Nothing is more comforting for a meat-eater than a meat loaf. Besides, the leftovers can be warmed up in a jiffy on a frying pan, and makes such good sandwiches. Of *course*, you have to have mashed potatoes with it. Maybe peas.

2 POUNDS OF GROUND BEEF

2 EGGS, BEATEN

2 CUPS BREADCRUMBS

5 TABLESPOONS FINELY-CHOPPED ONIONS

1 TEASPOON SALT

1 TEASPOON PEPPER

¼ TEASPOON DRY MUSTARD

¼ TEASPOON CHILI POWDER

¼ TEASPOON FINELY CRUMBLED SAGE

½ CUP TOMATO PUREE

½ CUP CELERY, FINELY CHOPPED

Heat the oven to 350 degrees. Mix all the ingredients together thoroughly in a large bowl. Pack into a loaf pan. Bake for one and a half-hours or until well-done. {Serves 8}

• • •

SKILLET SUPPER OF CHICKEN AND RICE OR COUSCOUS

Cooked in a cast iron skillet, this supper goes together quickly and messes up only one pan. Start it forty-five minutes ahead of supper time and once it's assembled, there's little more to do. Chicken thighs or legs are best, bone in. Rice or couscous picks up all the flavors. Greens like arugula, spinach, or shredded chard steam on top of the full pan.

This is an eminently flexible meal. Adjust the number of thighs you have to the number of diners; adjust the onion size to the thighs or your taste; use a wider pan and add more rice or couscous when you cook more thighs. Start with equal amounts of rice or pasta and hot water, adding gradually more as it cooks and the liquid is absorbed.

1 MEDIUM TO LARGE ONION

OLIVE OIL

1 CHICKEN THIGH PER PERSON

¼ TO ⅓ CUP RICE OR SMALL PASTA PER PERSON

½ TO ⅔ CUP OF HOT WATER OR STOCK PER PERSON

1 TEASPOON OF FAVORITE SEASONING OR COMBINATION OF SEASONINGS

A GENEROUS HANDFUL OF TENDER GREENS PER PERSON

SALT AND PEPPER

Slice the onion, put a little olive oil in a skillet over a medium heat, and cook the onion until it is soft and translucent, five minutes at least. Push the onion to one side and lay the thighs

{ADVICE}

» To season your skillet chicken, if you like Tex-Mex flavors, then chili powder, cumin, and chipotle powder will be your seasoning, topped perhaps with cilantro. Indian? Cook with curry or garam masala and serve with chutney on top. Italian? Garlic, oregano, basil, marjoram, thyme, and red pepper flakes, and grate a lot of parmesan on top. Moroccan? Ras al Hanout with a few stewed tomatoes mixed in. You get the picture. Or maybe all you want to taste is chicken, so salt and pepper will do the trick.

skin side down to brown five to ten minutes, raising the heat a little if necessary. When the skin has a golden color, flip it over and cook the thighs for another five minutes. Sprinkle the rice or pasta all around the chicken and add the hot water or stock. It will bubble vigorously at first, then settle down to a simmer. Adjust the heat to simmer. Sprinkle the seasonings over the top of the chicken and rice or pasta. Add salt and pepper to taste, and put a lid on the skillet. Simmer the dish for about a half hour. Check to see if it needs more liquid and test for doneness. (Juices from chicken should run clear.) Lay the greens over the top of the chicken and grains, return the lid, and leave for another five minutes or until the greens are wilted.

. . .

Sautéed Duck Breast with Tart Fruit Sauce

Duck, like goose, is a fatty little number, and the chunk of skin that comes attached to a duck breast is partly the reason we enjoy eating it, providing you cook it so that much of the oily part is rendered out, and the skin crisps up nicely. The other thing to keep in mind about duck is that, like steak, a little pink in the flesh is a good thing. Cook it medium rare.

Tart fruit sauce cuts through some of the fattiness of duck. If you can find currant jelly, use that; any bitter orange or lemon marmalade, used with garlic and shallots, should give you the requisite sour element, though you'll see apricot, peach, and cherry preserves recommended sometimes.

1 DUCK BREAST
1 SHALLOT CHOPPED
1 CLOVE OF GARLIC, MINCED FINELY
3 TO 4 TABLESPOONS OF TART FRUIT PRESERVE

Score the duck breast skin in a cross-hatched pattern, avoiding cutting into the meat. Heat a heavy frying pan or griddle on high, and lay the breast on it, skin side down. Reduce the heat to medium-low and cook for eight to twelve minutes. Turn the breast over and cook for two to three minutes. If you want to finish it on the grill, heat the grill, and put the breast on it for about three to four minutes, otherwise cook the breast for another three minutes in the pan; then set it aside to rest while you make the sauce. Drain most of the duck fat from the frying pan, retaining a tablespoon or two in the pan. Add the shallots and garlic to the fat and cook for a minute or two, then add the preserves, stirring to mix the shallots and garlic with the melting preserve. Set aside. Slice the duck breast thinly and dribble the sauce over it. Serve warm to room temperature. *{Serves 2}*

• • •

SHEET PAN HONEY MUSTARD CHICKEN AND VEGETABLES

Sheet pan dinners—a whole meal baked or roasted on a single flat baking pan—probably has more of us fixing dinner at home in preference to take out or using pre made frozen dinners. Assembly time is minimal, baking takes thirty to forty-five minutes, then it is time to serve. One pan to clean up, and if you plan for it, you might have some toothsome leftovers.

Calculate quantities needed on the number of diners, remembering a teenager might like two pieces of chicken and a lot of potato while an older person might prefer a small piece of chicken and half a potato.

CHICKEN PIECES, PREFERABLY BONE IN, AND SKIN ON
WHITE POTATO, PEELED AND CUT INTO CHUNKS
SWEET POTATO CUT INTO CHUNKS
CARROTS, PEELED AND CUT INTO THICK SLICES
ONIONS, PEELED AND HALVED, OR QUARTERED IF LARGE
DIJON-STYLE MUSTARD, GRAINY OR SMOOTH
HONEY
BALSAMIC VINEGAR

Heat the oven to 400 degrees. Lightly oil a baking pan or sheet pan. Arrange the chicken pieces on the pan, skin side up. Toss the vegetable chunks in a bowl with a little oil until they glisten and add them to the baking pan. Sprinkle all with some salt and pepper. Mix together the honey and the mustard, sampling

{ADVICE}

» *How to make honey mustard? Decide if you want grainy or smooth mustard. Spoon a couple of tablespoons out of the mustard jar of your choice into a small bowl. Add honey a spoonful at a time, tasting as you go until it tastes right to you. Don't worry about specific quantities because different mustards vary in their intensity.*

until it tastes good to you, then drip in some balsamic mixture to achieve a thin sauce. Smear all the ingredients in the pan with honey mustard and balsamic sauce. Roast for thirty-five to forty-five minutes, turning the vegetables at least once and checking for an internal temperature of 165 degrees on the thighs. Serve. *{Makes a variable number of servings}*

. . .

Hearty Braised Short Ribs

When we have snow and ice underfoot, and cold wind whistling around our ears, that's the perfect time for rich, hearty beef short ribs. If you use well-marbled meat, they'll render their own fat when you brown them; if yours are a little lean, add a small amount of olive oil in the pan to get them started. Salt, pepper, thyme, and pureed garlic distributed over the ribs, with chicken stock and red wine added, and a tight lid on the pot, the ribs simmer away for a couple of hours and make dinner while you do other things.

Be sure to use your heaviest-bottomed cooking pot for these ribs braised on top of the stove at low, or in a 275 degree oven, for the two to three hours needed to achieve tender meat.

3 POUNDS OF BEEF SHORT RIBS AT ROOM TEMPERATURE

OLIVE OIL

SALT AND PEPPER

2 TEASPOONS CRUMBLED THYME

2 TO 3 CLOVES OF GARLIC PUREED

½ CUP OR MORE RED WINE

2 CUPS OF CHICKEN STOCK

12 SMALL ONIONS, PEELED, LEFT WHOLE

2 CUPS SLICED MUSHROOMS

Over a medium high heat, first sear the bone ends of the ribs until dark brown, salting and peppering as you go. Sear the sides, salting and peppering the uncooked side, and turning as each side develops a dark, roasted color. Distribute crumbled thyme and pureed garlic over the ribs, pour red wine over them and simmer for a few moments, then add the chicken stock until the ribs are surrounded but not covered in stock. Simmer at a low, steady temperature for about two hours, checking to make sure they do not dry out. Cook until they are fork tender. Sauté the mushrooms and brown the onions and set aside to add to the ribs for the last twenty minutes before serving. *{Serves 4 to 6}*

· · ·

Hearty Lentil and Sausage Supper

Lentils are so adaptable and wholesome, and so darn homely. Good hot in soups, curried in Indian-style dal, and a good addition to cold salads. Cheap, too, high in fiber, lots of minerals, nutrient-dense, and muddy-looking on a plate. To make up for lentils' looks, make sure they are really flavorful.

2 CUPS DRIED LENTILS

SAUSAGE TO TASTE (GARLIC, ITALIAN MILD OR HOT, KIELBASA)

1 LARGE ONION

2 CLOVES OF FINELY CHOPPED GARLIC

2 TO 3 TABLESPOONS OLIVE OIL

1½ TO 2 CUPS STEWED TOMATOES WITH SAUCE

1 TABLESPOON SMOKED PAPRIKA, OR TO TASTE

1 TEASPOON OR SEVERAL FRESH GRINDS OF BLACK PEPPER

RED PEPPER FLAKES TO TASTE, OPTIONAL

Cover the lentils with three to four cups of water and bring to a boil, then reduce the heat and simmer for 15 to 20 minutes or until they are tender. Set aside. In a heavy skillet or pot, sauté the onion in olive oil until just soft, about five minutes, and add garlic and cook another minute or so. Drain the lentils, reserving the water, and add them to the onion and garlic mixture. Add the tomatoes and sauce, paprika, pepper, and other seasonings to taste, distributing them evenly. You should see liquid among the lentils, and if you don't, add some reserved cooking water. Simmer onions, lentil and tomatoes together over a low heat, while in another pan you fry the sausage until browned. Leave sausages whole or cut up, as you wish, and add them to the lentils to cook together a while longer, about a half hour, adding more lentil cooking water if the lentils absorb the moisture.
{Serves 2 to 4 depending on the amount of sausage used}

...

Smoked Haddock, Mashed Potatoes, and Cheddar

We often celebrate St. Patrick's Day with corned beef and cabbage but Irish cooking has lots of other great food and lots in common with traditional Maine cooking. A small country surrounded by the sea, Irish menus feature oysters, salmon, and periwinkles and like the rest of the British Isles, smoked haddock, which some of us know by the name Finnan Haddie (haddock from Findon, Scotland.)

Granted, smoked haddock can be a bit pricey. It isn't always available in the seafood department of grocery stores, though many fish markets keep it on hand. If this recipe appeals, you might acquire your fish when you see it, then freeze it until you're ready to make a meal out of it.

1 MEDIUM POTATO PER SERVING

2 TABLESPOONS OF BUTTER

1 SMALL SLICED ONION PER PERSON, OR 1 MEDIUM ONION FOR
    TWO OR THREE SERVINGS

3½ TO 4 OUNCES OF SMOKED HADDOCK PER PERSON

CREAM SUFFICIENT TO NEARLY COVER THE FISH

2 OR 3 GRATINGS OF NUTMEG, OR TO TASTE

SALT AND PEPPER, TO TASTE

1 OUNCE OF GRATED CHEDDAR PER PERSON, OR MORE OR LESS TO TASTE

PARSLEY OR SCALLIONS TO TASTE.

Boil the potatoes, and when they are tender remove from the heat, drain, and set aside. Meanwhile, melt the butter in a skillet on a medium heat and add the onion, cooking it until it is softened; then remove it from the pan and set it aside. Put the fish and cream into the skillet and simmer for about ten minutes until it flakes apart. Add the nutmeg. Mash the potatoes, adding a little butter and cream from the skillet holding the fish. Fold in the fish, onions, and a little cheddar and enough remaining cream to create a moist mixture. Stir in the parsley or scallions. Spoon into a baking dish or ramekins, top with more grated cheese and broil until the top is bubbly and golden colored. {Makes variable number of servings}

. . .

Sweet Italian Sausage Ragu

The flavor of this ragu depends on the quality of the sausage. Use your favorite sweet sausage in casing, by slitting the skin open and removing the meat, or acquire bulk sausage. A combination of aromatics—onion, carrot, celery, and garlic—often the base for soups and sauces, really helps gets the ragu off to a great start.

Adding dry white wine to the mixture as it cooks also jacks up the flavor. It doesn't take much, and the cook and friends can always drink whatever doesn't go into the sauce.

1 RIB CELERY

1 MEDIUM CARROT

1 MEDIUM ONION

1 CLOVE GARLIC

4 TABLESPOONS OLIVE OIL

SPRINKLE OF SALT

1 POUND SWEET ITALIAN SAUSAGE

1 CUP WHITE WINE

1 CUP TOMATO SAUCE

1 TEASPOON FENNEL SEED (OPTIONAL)

SALT AND PEPPER

Using a box or similar grater, grate the celery, onion, carrot, and garlic. Put olive oil into a heavy pot over a medium heat and when it shimmers, add the grated vegetables. Sprinkle lightly with salt and cook for about five minutes, stirring to prevent sticking. Slit the sausages and remove the meat, adding it to the vegetables, and breaking it up into small pieces. Add the wine and stir to combine. Let cook for ten minutes or so while the meat absorbs the wine. Add more wine if it tends to cook dry. Add the tomato sauce, stir, and cook for another twenty minutes or so. Sample and add salt and pepper to taste. If you wish a stronger fennel flavor, toast the fennel seeds until they are aromatic. Grind in a grinder or with mortar and pestle and add to the sauce. Use immediately with your favorite pasta cooked according to the instructions on the package, or store for use later.

Maple Mustard Glazed Pork Roast with Cider

Choose a boneless loin roast with a fairly thin layer of fat left on top. Brine it in a mixture of cider and salt with mustard seeds, peppercorns, and bay leaves added to help keep the meat tender and moist.

A glaze made with mustard, maple syrup, and brown sugar finishes the pork beautifully, and there may be enough to spread on cut slices of meat as sauce.

1 4- TO 5-POUND BONELESS PORK ROAST

SALT AND PEPPER

VEGETABLE OIL

½ CUP DIJON-STYLE OR GRAINY MUSTARD

⅓ CUP LIGHT BROWN SUGAR

2 TABLESPOONS DARK MAPLE SYRUP

1 CUP OF CIDER OR APPLE JUICE

SALT AND PEPPER

VEGETABLE OIL

½ CUP DIJON-STYLE OR GRAINY MUSTARD

⅓ CUP LIGHT BROWN SUGAR

2 TABLESPOONS DARK MAPLE SYRUP

1 CUP OF CIDER OR APPLE JUICE

Heat the oven to 400 degrees. Sprinkle the pork all over lightly with salt and several grinds of black pepper. Heat a little oil in a heavy frying pan and brown the meat on all sides. Place the pork in a baking dish or roasting pan. Mix together the mustard, brown sugar, and maple syrup in a small bowl. Spread the mustard mixture all over the roast, top and sides. Pour a cup of cider into the dish or pan, just about enough to cover the bottom. Roast the pork for about an hour, spreading a fresh layer of mustard mixture about halfway through the roasting time. Test the roast for an interior temperature of 140 degrees (or more if you prefer.) Use extra mustard mixture as a condiment on the roasted meat.

{ADVICE}

≪ If you decide to go the brining route, combine half a cup of kosher salt with a quarter cup of brown sugar, two cups of cider, and one cup of water. Add a tablespoon each of peppercorns, mustard seeds, and a bay leaf. Heat it until the salt and sugar dissolves, then cool completely. Add your roast, and leave it in the brine, turning it occasionally for about eight hours (overnight is fine, too). Some people put the meat and brine in a zip-closing plastic bag for the process.

When you are ready to cook the meat, take it out of the brine, dry the surface with a paper towel, and let it sit for at least a half hour before proceeding with glazing and baking.

3
SUMMER SUPPERS AND SUMMER LUNCHES

Some days, it's too darn hot and humid to cook, even on a grill outdoors. Cool food is the only answer, and homecooked because who wants to change clothes, climb into a hot car, and drive somewhere to eat outside in the humidity and heat? Other days, we might feel like cooking as long as it doesn't take too long, because fine summer weather beckons us outdoors. Then, too, lots of folks, including our own nearest and dearest, make Maine their vacation destination, so we find ourselves coming up with meals for hungry visitors.

The good news: look at all the wonderful fresh vegetables at farm stands, farmers markets, even chain grocery stores. Maybe you collect a box of vegetables from a community supported agriculture (CSA) program near you. Or maybe you have a garden a stone's throw from your kitchen door where fresh vegetables abound.

Summer cooking needs strategies.

Quick Meals

*U*se these strategies for quick meals.

Keep cooked pasta or potatoes on hand to turn into a cold salad at a moment's notice with leftover vegetables and meat and salad dressing.

Keep vegetables like cucumbers; bell peppers in green, red, and orange; carrots; snap peas; celery washed, peeled when necessary and cut into handy snack-worthy size are great pick-me-ups with a favorite dip (as easy as pesto stirred into a little mayonnaise). Sturdier vegetables like broccoli, cauliflower, and green beans benefit from a quick one-minute blanche in hot water to bring out their flavor before adding them to the crudites platter or chopping into salad.

A whole roasted chicken, besides making dinner one day, provides, with little preparation, fillings for sandwiches, salad, tacos, and quesadillas for a few more days.

Dessert? How about the no-churn ice cream that wants only a 14-ounce can of sweetened condensed milk with a couple of tablespoons of bourbon or vanilla to taste stirred into it, then a pint of whipping cream beaten and folded into the milk? Want chocolate flavor? Stir a bit of cocoa powder into the milk, or even some instant coffee, then add the whipped cream. Put the mixture into a container with a lid and freeze it. Start early in the day and by evening you'll have your ice cream.

Feeling too hot and lazy to whip cream? How about fresh strawberries, raspberries or blueberries with a pour of cream and a sprinkle of sugar? Delicious.

. . .

Mediterranean-Inspired Pasta Salad

Penne, raddiatore, farfalle, shells, gemelli, and even mini-raviolis and tortellini work well in this free-for-all salad. You get to decide what your pasta to vegetable ratio will be. If you feel clueless about this, start with at least a half a cup of pasta per person, plus one for the bowl. With the rest of the ingredients, use as much as you like. Leave out anything you don't like.

½ CUP PER PERSON OF PENNE OR OTHER SHORT PASTA,
    COOKED AND COOLED
CUCUMBER LIGHTLY PEELED AND DICED
MINCED SHALLOT OR SCALLIONS WHITE AND TENDER
    GREEN PARTS, CHOPPED
KALAMATA OLIVES, PITTED AND CHOPPED
FRESH RED PEPPER OR ROASTED OR GRILLED RED PEPPERS IN OIL,
CHOPPED
ARTICHOKE HEARTS, CHOPPED
CHERRY TOMATOES, HALVED, TO TASTE
FETA CHEESE, CRUMBLED, TO TASTE
TUNA, CANNED, TO TASTE, OPTIONAL
VINAIGRETTE DRESSING
WASHED AND TORN LETTUCE

Toss together the pasta, cucumber, shallot or scallions, olives, red pepper, feta, tomatoes and tuna. Add the vinaigrette, tossing the salad and sampling until the flavor suits you. Add salt and pepper to taste. Distribute the lettuce on plates for each person and spoon the dressed salad on top. {*Serves a variable number of people*}

• • •

Marinated Cucumbers and Onions

One cool summer comfort includes a marinated cucumber and onion mixture with sweet and sour brine. A pretty steady occupant of the fridge most summer weeks at our house, it's perfect for forking onto a plate alongside nearly anything. If you have a mandolin, this is a good time to use it, or a slicing blade in the food processor.

1 CUP CIDER VINEGAR
1 CUP SUGAR
¼ TEASPOON SALT
2 CUCUMBERS, SLICED THINLY
1 SMALL ONION, SLICED THINLY
WATER

Stir the vinegar, sugar, and salt together until the sugar and salt are dissolved. Pour the vinegar mixture over the sliced vegetables in a bowl or large jar. Add just enough water to cover the vegetables. Chill in the fridge for a few hours so the flavors develop.

. . .

Lettuce, Tomato, and Cucumber Salad

Summer is lettuce time. Go ahead and tear up all that nice, crisp lettuce straight from the garden, farmer's market, or produce section of the grocery store. Piles of it, perhaps a mix of green and red lettuces and other greens if you like them, like arugula, sprouts, spinach, baby kale. When tomatoes ripen and cucumbers fruit abundantly, we can make the finest salads of the year.

This salad is nearly self-dressing. The diced tomato and cucumber lightly salted, put in a small bowl with about a spoon-sized blob of mayonnaise, gets a quick stir and is set aside. The tomato and cucumber yield up their juices and make a flavorful dressing when distributed over lettuce and tossed.

If you don't want to use mayo, though with this method you need hardly any, add a mere shake or two of red wine vinegar and a scant tablespoon of olive oil to the salted and peppered tomatoes and cucumbers.

1 MEDIUM TOMATO
½ SLICING CUCUMBER
SALT AND PEPPER
1 SMALL SPOONFUL OF MAYONNAISE
1 HEAD OF LETTUCE

Dice the tomato and cucumber both into small cubes, a put into a small bowl. Add sprinkle of salt and pepper, stir, then add the mayonnaise and stir again. Set aside. Tear the lettuce into bite-sized pieces into a salad bowl. At serving time, distribute the tomato and cucumber with their juices over the lettuce and toss.

. . .

Fennel Salad

Fennel bulbs, white at the bottom with feathery, dark green fronds, reminiscent of dill, are available year-round in the grocery store and often at farmer's markets. Not everyone likes a vegetable that tastes like licorice, though they might really enjoy a slight burst of that flavor when they eat a sweet Italian sausage or certain fennel-studded salamis. Fennel flavor is light and the texture is crunchy when shredded.

To slice fennel, a mandolin really is a terrific tool. It shaves the bulb thinly and regularly. A food processor slicing blade might work, too, if you avoid pressing the fennel bulb too firmly into the feeding tube because thin shreds are best. Otherwise, a good chef knife will do it.

SHAVED FENNEL SALAD WITH LEMON AND OLIVE OIL

1 FENNEL BULB

ZEST OF HALF A LEMON

1 TABLESPOON OLIVE OIL

½ TEASPOON TOASTED FENNEL SEEDS, OPTIONAL

SALT AND PEPPER TO TASTE

Shave the fennel bulb thinly and scatter over a platter, two to three slices deep. Sprinkle about half the lemon zest on the fennel shreds and add the remaining zest to the olive oil in a separate small bowl. Let stand for an hour. Dribble the oil over the shaved fennel. Sprinkle the optional fennel seeds over the shaved fennel. Add a light sprinkle of salt and pepper. Toss just before serving.

. . .

Tuna and Cannellini Salad with Lemon Vinaigrette

If you keep canned tuna and cannellini beans on hand in your pantry, this substantial salad is just a can-opener away. Can sizes are an ever-shifting proposition, as the food industry shaves an ounce off the contents every so often. Still, a large can of tuna will hold nine ounces of tuna after draining. A thirteen-ounce can of cannellini will be close to two cups. If you decide to soak dry cannellini and cook them up yourself, aim for a scant two cups. These two cans full will be a good proportion of tuna to beans, though you should suit yourself; add more tuna if you wish, or more beans.

JUICE OF 1 LEMON

3 TABLESPOONS OLIVE OIL

2 CLOVES OF GARLIC, MINCED

SALT AND PEPPER TO TASTE

1 13-OUNCE CAN OF CANNELLINI BEANS, RINSED WELL,
    OR 1¾ CUPS COOKED CANNELLINI

1 9-OUNCE CAN CHUNK LIGHT TUNA

½ MEDIUM RED ONION, CHOPPED

1 TABLESPOON CAPERS, DRAINED

CHERRY TOMATOES, HALVED, TO TASTE

2 TO 3 SPRIGS PARSLEY, MINCED

6 TO 7 BASIL LEAVES, SHREDDED

LETTUCE WASHED AND TORN

Put the lemon juice, olive oil, and garlic into a medium-sized shallow bowl and whisk together. Add salt and pepper and taste, adjusting seasonings if necessary. Add all the rest of the ingredients and toss gently until the dressing is well-distributed. Serve on a bed of lettuce.

• • •

ASPARAGUS SOUP

Lightly steamed, served with butter, salt and pepper, the first fresh asparagus of the season tastes divine. Later, as the supply continues, you might want to experiment with pasta and asparagus, roasted asparagus, or asparagus cooked and chopped into salads, or made into soup as follows.

OLIVE OIL

1 MEDIUM ONION, CHOPPED

4 TO 6 STALKS ASPARAGUS PER PERSON, CHOPPED INTO ONE-INCH PIECES

CHICKEN OR VEGETABLE BROTH, OR WATER
SALT AND PEPPER
MILK, CREAM, EVAPORATED MILK, HALF-AND-HALF, OPTIONAL
SHERRY TO TASTE, OPTIONAL

Heat the olive oil in a heavy bottomed soup pot over a medium heat. Add the chopped onion. Cook for about five minutes then add the asparagus pieces and sauté them for five minutes, or until they turn bright green. Add the broth until the asparagus is covered; bring to a boil, then reduce the heat to a simmer. Cook the vegetable until it is tender, ten or more minutes depending on the size of the asparagus. Taste and add salt and pepper. Serve, or continue with the following directions for a cream soup. Gradually add milk, cream, evaporated milk, or half-and-half to taste, and bring back up to temperature over a low heat. Taste and adjust seasonings. Add the optional sherry, starting with a couple of tablespoons and adding more to your taste. Puree for a smooth soup, if desired. *{Makes a variable number of servings}*

· · ·

Zucchini Soup

Fast, simple, delicious, and wholesome, this recipe came from Ruth Thurston in Machias. When zucchinis squirt from plants in the garden, we welcome having a way to use four cups of diced zuke at a whack. Ruth wrote that she used frozen zucchini, so if you don't want to make this now, chunk up your zucchini and freeze it in three to four cup amounts to use later.

Ruth observed that the soup needs more than just a dash of the seasonings. Absolutely. No wimpy little sprinkles here: use a generous quantity of dill and curry.

The cream cheese makes it rich and creamy. You could try using ricotta, cottage cheese, or goat cheese, or even generous globs of sour cream. If you wish something low-fat, try Neufchatel, or plain, Greek-style, yogurt.

Use chicken stock instead of bouillon cubes or, for vegetarians, vegetable broth or miso paste.

You can make this soup quickly, in half an hour. If you put

hot stuff in a blender or food processor, it might puree explosively. Use a stick blender if you have one. Otherwise allow the cooked squash mixture to cool a bit before pureeing.

1 MEDIUM LARGE ZUCCHINI, OR ABOUT 4 CUPS CHOPPED

2 CUPS WATER

2 CHICKEN BOUILLON CUBES OR VEGETABLE BOUILLON

2 CLOVES OF PEELED GARLIC LEFT WHOLE

1 TABLESPOON CRUSHED DRIED DILL

1 HEAPING TEASPOON CURRY POWDER, OR TO TASTE

BLACK PEPPER TO TASTE

4 OUNCES CREAM CHEESE SOFTENED TO ROOM TEMPERATURE

Put the zucchini, water, bouillon, and garlic in a medium pan, bring to a boil and cook until the zucchini is soft, about fifteen minutes. Stir in the dill, curry powder and pepper. Add the cream cheese and stir until it is mostly melted. Taste and adjust seasonings. Puree and serve.

• • •

CABBAGE FRITTER

Neighbors down the road, Roger and Marny Heinen, like cabbage fritter for lunch, though it could be supper for vegetarian (or any other) households, or an ample side dish. Grill a couple of sausages or offer ham to go with it. Sprinkle it with cooked chopped bacon. Cheese on top is lovely and optional. Think about a salad on the side, or maybe simply sliced tomatoes. The cabbage becomes quite tender, and the top turns a golden brown.

½ SMALL CABBAGE, SLICED THINLY

1 SMALL ONION SLICED THINLY

½ CUP OF FLOUR

3 EGGS, BEATEN

VEGETABLE OIL

GRATED CHEESE, TO TASTE

SALT AND PEPPER

Put the shredded cabbage and onion in a large bowl. Add the flour and toss to distribute it through the cabbage and onion. Add the beaten eggs and mix in. Season to taste with salt and pepper. Grease a large frying pan with a bit of oil and put the vegetable mixture in. Cover very tightly with a lid or foil. Cook for 10 to 12 minutes on medium low heat. Flip and add grated cheese, continue cooking until cheese melts and the bottom is browned. *{Serves 4 to 6}*

• • •

Tomato and Corn Salad

Cooked corn, possibly even better grilled, and a fairly equal quantity each of corn and tomatoes, with lime juice to taste, and only enough olive oil to pull the flavors together makes a grand salad. Garnish with a little chopped cilantro. So good!

3 LARGE TOMATOES
3 EARS OF CORN, BOILED OR GRILLED
1 SMALL RED ONION, FINELY CHOPPED
JUICE OF 1 LIME, MORE OR LESS TO TASTE
OLIVE OIL
SALT AND PEPPER TO TASTE

Peel and coarsely chop the tomatoes, put them in a bowl. Cut the corn from the cobs and add to the tomatoes. Add the onion. Add the lime juice gradually, mixing and tasting to suit yourself. Dribble in some olive oil. Add salt and pepper, stir to mix, taste and adjust seasoning.

• • •

Cold Vegetable Pizza with Spicy Peanut Sauce

Pre-baked pizza crust, or dough that you bake at home, gets you off to a start on this cold pizza. The sauce is very similar to the one used for chicken satay, or Pad Thai, or one I use for plain pasta. If you already have a favorite peanut sauce recipe, by all means use it.

Giving this pizza a little needed oomph is easily accomplished by serving it with bottled hot sauce on the table so that an individual diner can ramp up the heat to personal taste.

If a vegetarian pizza won't work in your household, add some cooked chicken or shrimp to the top of this and you'll be all set.

⅓ CUP OF SMOOTH PEANUT BUTTER

2 TABLESPOONS SOY SAUCE

2 TABLESPOONS RICE VINEGAR

2 TABLESPOONS HONEY

1 TEASPOON FRESH GINGER, MINCED, OR DRIED POWDERED TO TASTE

2 CLOVES GARLIC, PEELED

1 THIN, 12-INCH PRE-BAKED PIZZA CRUST

½ LARGE RED PEPPER, DICED FINELY

1 LARGE CARROT, PEELED AND SHREDDED COARSELY

1 CUP FRESH BEAN SPROUTS

2 TO 3 SCALLIONS WHITE AND GREEN PARTS, THINLY SLICED

FRESH CILANTRO, FINELY CHOPPED OR SHREDDED

CHOPPED PEANUTS

Mix the peanut butter, soy sauce, rice vinegar, ginger together and add pureed garlic. Spread evenly over the pizza crust. Sprinkle evenly the red pepper, shredded carrots, and bean sprouts. Top with sliced scallions, cilantro, and chopped peanuts. Serve with hot sauce, if desired.

• • •

Mary's Quick Lunch

Islesboro's summer community, which has been turning up on the island for over a hundred years, with Linda Gillies' capable and judicious editing, produced a charming and beautiful community cookbook called *Summer Food*. Summer residents sent recipes along with memories for dishes they make when they are on island for the summer.

One, "Mary's Quick Lunch," submitted by one of Mary Homan's daughters, reminded us that Mary was a wonderful flower gardener, and liked to go boating in the summer. Anyone can understand why she wanted to have a tasty, fast lunch to serve guests, if she had any, and then get right back outdoors.

Mary served this lovely cheesy-eggy thing with a salad and tomatoes. Apparently, it makes good appetizers on toast rounds, too.

3 HARD-BOILED EGGS, CHOPPED

8 OUNCES OF GRATED CHEDDAR CHEESE

2 TO 3 SCALLIONS OR GREEN ONIONS CHOPPED FINELY

MAYONNAISE

SALT AND PEPPER

6 SLICES OF BREAD

Mix the eggs, cheese, and onions with just enough mayonnaise to make a stiff but spreadable mixture. Add salt and pepper to taste. Toast the bread slices on one side under the broiler. Take them out of the broiler, turn them over, spread the egg and cheese mixture rather thickly to the edges. Broil for four to five minutes until bubbly and brown on top. Serve immediately. {Serves 6}

• • •

Salmon Burgers with Herby Garlic Sauce

Start with uncooked salmon that you grind in a food processor and add dry bread crumbs or panko to keep the fish from being too sticky. For a crunchy exterior, press the burgers into panko-style crumbs on each side before cooking them in a fry pan with butter and olive oil. Make patties about an inch thick, cook them until they are medium rare, just like beef burgers, or, if you prefer, until they are thoroughly done. Do it all to taste.

You can assemble and refrigerate these burgers for a day or so before cooking them. A pound and a half of fresh salmon makes four six-ounce burgers which is a hearty size for dinner, but it could just as well create satisfying servings of six four-ounce burgers. By the way, the salmon mix would make lots and lots of bite-sized appetizers.

{ADVICE}

« CRAB CAKES
Making salmon cakes reminded me of how I make crab cakes: I puree a piece of plain white fish then add picked crab. The fish takes up the crab flavor and holds the crab meat together so I don't have to use a lot of egg or bread crumbs to bind it. I dip each crab cake into crumbs and cook them as I do the salmon cakes.

1½ POUNDS FRESH SALMON

2 WHOLE SHALLOTS OR 1 SMALL MILD ONION, CUT INTO CHUNKS

¾ CUP DRIED COARSE BREADCRUMBS

SALT AND PEPPER

PANKO-STYLE BREADCRUMBS, OPTIONAL

OLIVE OIL AND BUTTER

Remove the skin from the salmon fillet and cut it into chunks about two inches square. Put about a quarter of the chunks into a food processor and grind it until it turns into a paste. Add the balance of the chunks and the shallot or onion and pulse it a few times until you see thumbnail-sized pieces of fish. Put the fish mixture into a bowl and add the bread-crumbs, and salt and pepper by stirring it all gently until mixed. Form the burgers about an inch thick. Put about two tablespoons of butter into a frying pan and add a couple of tablespoons of olive oil. Heat it over medium high until it is quite hot and bubbles a little. Add the burgers and fry on one side for about two and a half minutes until golden, then turn over and fry another two to three minutes. Make a little slit to test for doneness. You may prefer to use a prepared tartar sauce or cocktail sauce with your salmon burgers, or make the sauce below.

HERBY GARLIC SAUCE

¾ CUP MAYONNAISE

1 CLOVE GARLIC, PUREED

1 TABLESPOON DILL, OR MORE TO TASTE

1 TABLESPOON CHOPPED CHIVES OR MORE TO TASTE

DAB OF CUCUMBER RELISH, OPTIONAL

SQUEEZE OF LEMON JUICE

Blend all ingredients together and taste, adding more of anything you prefer.

CHICKEN (OR CRAB) AND CORN QUESADILLAS

This Tex-Mex recipe came a couple years ago from one Josephine Belknap. The original recipe called for crab, but Josephine crossed out the word crab and added chicken instead and *that* caught my eye. If you like crab, then, by all means, use this recipe with it, but the quesadillas with chicken are tasty and a bit more affordable.

¼ CUP (2 OUNCES) CREAM CHEESE
JUICE OF HALF A LIME
¼ TEASPOON CUMIN, OR TO TASTE
2 TO 3 SCALLIONS CHOPPED
1 TABLESPOON CHOPPED CILANTRO
1 CUP COOKED CORN KERNELS
1 CUP COOKED SHREDDED CHICKEN OR CRAB
4 8-INCH FLOUR TORTILLAS
SHREDDED MONTEREY JACK CHEESE

Mix together the cream cheese, lime juice, cumin, scallions, and cilantro. Add the corn and chicken or crab and blend. Warm the tortillas gently on a griddle and spread a quarter or less of the chicken or crab and corn mixture on half of the tortilla. Sprinkle the cheese over the mixture and fold the tortilla together. Toast both sides on a griddle, or warm briefly in an oven. Serve warm.

• • •

MISSISSIPPI ROAST

This ingenious recipe works with beef, pork, and chicken. It'll taste good any time of year, can be cooked in a slow cooker, slow oven, or on the stove top in a Dutch oven without much attention from the cook. You can serve the results lots of ways. It will remind you of pulled pork, only with the perky flavor of pepperoncini, a pickled pepper easily found in the grocery store.

The original recipe, contributed by Robin Chapman of Ripley, Mississippi to a community cookbook, was subsequently picked up by a blogger, whizzed around the internet for a while, and

>> *Quite a bit of this dish can be prepared ahead of time, one of the reasons that Gayle Foster, who summers here on Islesboro, likes this recipe. If you have roasted a chicken, the leftover meat is perfect when picked off, and cut up, or you can cook chicken thighs or breasts for it. Gayle wrote, "I usually cook a hen for dinner the week I make this and add the leftover chicken from that."*

The rice ought to be cooked a day ahead and left to improve overnight. Gayle likes to use fresh grated ginger when she can get it, prefers yogurt to sour cream, and likes to garnish with toasted, slivered almonds. She pointed out that you can add water chestnuts and more green pepper, if you wish.

Then assemble it and serve. Gayle recommends a bed of lettuce, and cherry tomatoes to decorate it.

cropped up in the *New York Times* where the packaged Ranch Dressing mix was converted into recognizable ingredients like mayonnaise, vinegar, buttermilk, dill, flour.

Serve this on a bun if you want, or a little pile of noodles, or alongside potatoes.

1 3- TO 4-POUND BONELESS CHUCK ROAST

SALT

PEPPER

FLOUR

VEGETABLE OIL

6 TABLESPOONS BUTTER

8 TO 12 PEPPERONCINI

2 TABLESPOONS MAYONNAISE

2 TEASPOONS CIDER VINEGAR

1 TEASPOON DRIED DILL

¼ TEASPOON PAPRIKA

1 TABLESPOON BUTTERMILK

Sprinkle the roast lightly with salt, pepper, and flour on all sides, and rub it all over. Put the vegetable oil in a heavy pan and bring to a high temperature. Sear the meat on all sides, enough to create a little crustiness, then put it into a slow cooker or Dutch oven with the butter and pepperoncini. Cover. Whisk together the mayonnaise, vinegar, dill, paprika and buttermilk until it is smooth, and add to the pot. If you use a slow cooker, set it at low; if you use a Dutch oven, keep the burner set at low. Cook for six to eight hours, or until you can shred it easily with a fork. Shred it and serve it with the pot gravy and pepperoncini poured over.

• • •

Gayle's Cold Curried Rice
with Chicken

This dish simply exudes the flavors of curry and chicken, studded with chunks of artichoke hearts, pitted black olives, and green peppers. More of a main dish than salad, serve it cold when the weather is hot, or room temperature when it's not, or even warmed up if it's chilly.

The curry is in the rice along with the bright tang of lemon juice. When you fold the chicken in with artichoke hearts, peppers, scallions, pitted black olives, and mayonnaise and yogurt or sour cream, the whole thing smooths out and the flavor deepens.

4 CUPS CHICKEN BROTH

2 CUPS UNCOOKED RICE

1 TEASPOON GROUND GINGER

2 TEASPOONS TO 1 TABLESPOON CURRY POWDER

½ TEASPOON TURMERIC

¼ CUP OLIVE OIL

JUICE OF 2 LEMONS

2 TO 3 CUPS COOKED CHICKEN MEAT, CUT SMALL

½ GREEN PEPPER CHOPPED SMALL

½ CUP SCALLIONS OR 1 SMALL RED ONION, OR TO TASTE

1 TO 1½ CUPS CHOPPED JARRED OR CANNED ARTICHOKE HEARTS,
    OR TO TASTE

PITTED, CHOPPED BLACK OLIVES TO TASTE, OPTIONAL

⅔ CUPS OF MAYONNAISE

⅔ CUP SOUR CREAM OR THICK YOGURT

2 TABLESPOONS TOASTED SLIVERED ALMONDS TO TASTE, OPTIONAL

LETTUCE AND CHERRY TOMATOES FOR GARNISH

Bring the chicken broth to a boil and add the rice along with the spices. Add salt to taste, depending on the saltiness of the broth. When the rice has absorbed all of the liquid, take off the heat and toss with the olive oil and lemon juice. Refrigerate overnight. Next day, add the chicken, green pepper, scallions or onion, and artichokes, plus optional olives, to the rice, and toss together. Mix the mayonnaise and sour cream or yogurt and fold into the rice and chicken. Taste and add more curry, or salt and pepper if desired. Make a bed of lettuce and spread the rice and chicken over it, garnish with cherry tomatoes and optional slivered almonds. {*Serves 6 to 8*}

Lobster Macaroni and Cheese

On most days, this is a special, wonderful company dish when we want to make sure our visiting friends get a taste of Maine lobster.

Two recipes follow: one produces a simple, serviceable dish; the other is more luxurious.

LOBSTER MACARONI AND CHEESE

1½ CUPS OF DRY PASTA, COOKED ACCORDING TO DIRECTIONS ON THE PACKAGE

2 BOILED LOBSTERS

2 TABLESPOONS BUTTER

2 TABLESPOONS FLOUR

1½ CUPS MILK

SALT AND PEPPER TO TASTE

1 CUP GRATED CHEDDAR CHEESE

NUTMEG, OPTIONAL, TO TASTE

BUTTERED BREAD CRUMBS, OPTIONAL

Pick out the lobster meat, and cut into bite sized pieces. Set aside. Melt the butter in a heavy pan, and stir in the flour, cooking over a medium heat until the flour and butter mixture bubbles and begins to thicken. Gradually whisk in the milk until the sauce is smooth and begins to thicken. Add salt, pepper, and nutmeg to taste. Stir in the cheddar and whisk until it melts and cook until it bubbles. Add a dash more milk if the sauce seems stiff. Stir in the cooked pasta and lobster, and heat through, adding more milk to keep the mixture soft enough to spoon. Taste and adjust seasonings. Serve from the pan, or if you wish to add a step, spoon into a baking dish, sprinkle on the buttered bread crumbs and bake at 350 degrees until hot, bubbly, and lightly browned. {Serves 4}

LUXURIOUS LOBSTER MAC AND CHEESE

1⅓ CUPS OF DRY PASTA COOKED ACCORDING TO DIRECTIONS ON THE PACKAGE

3 BOILED LOBSTERS

2 TO 3 TABLESPOONS BUTTER

2 TABLESPOONS FLOUR

2 CUPS CREAM OR HALF-AND-HALF

SALT AND PEPPER TO TASTE

1 CUP GRATED FONTINA CHEESE

½ CUP GRATED PARMESAN OR ROMANO CHEESE

SHERRY, OPTIONAL, TO TASTE

NUTMEG, OPTIONAL, TO TASTE

BUTTERED BREADCRUMBS, OPTIONAL

Pick out the lobster meat, and cut into bite-sized pieces. Set aside. Melt the butter in a heavy pan, and stir in the flour, cooking over a medium heat until the flour and butter mixture bubbles and begins to thicken. Gradually whisk in the cream until the sauce is smooth and begins to thicken. Add salt, pepper, nutmeg, and sherry to taste. Stir in the fontina and parmesan and whisk until it melts and cook until it bubbles. Add a dash more cream if the sauce seems stiff. Stir in the cooked pasta and lobster, and heat through, adding more milk to keep the mixture soft enough to spoon. Taste and adjust seasonings. Serve from the pan, or if you wish to add the step, spoon into a baking dish, sprinkle on the buttered breadcrumbs and bake at 350 degrees until hot, bubbly, and lightly browned. {Serves 4}

{ADVICE}

« *A relatively plain lobster mac and cheese made with a cream sauce and mild cheddar results in a perfectly delicious dish. Using a somewhat costlier cheese like Fontina or mozzarella cheese, and more of it; cream instead of milk; and adding sherry really jacks up the flavor and luxuriousness generally. When you consider the milk portion of the sauce, bear in mind the whole range of richness from milk to heavy cream, with half-and-half and light cream in between.*

Obviously, a higher proportion of lobster to pasta results in a richer dish, too. Small shell pasta and radiatore instead of elbow macaroni looks prettier and does not outsize the bites of lobster. Three-quarters as many lobsters as eaters provides enough lobster meat. For a group of four, three lobsters make for a generous serving of lobster while half a lobster per person makes a perfectly decent lobster mac and cheese. Add as little or as much pasta as you wish.

4
Good Morning

Time for breakfast, everyone.

Most of us have an extraordinary tolerance for repetitive breakfasts. We wouldn't dream of eating the same thing for supper every night, but at breakfast, we reach for the same foods day after day, after day. Perhaps we are clearing the fog of sleep from our minds and it just takes too much effort to dream up something different to eat at the same time.

We might shift breakfast offerings when company descends, especially in summer when friends, children, and grandchildren visit and must be fed. While we are content with a piece of toast and a cup of coffee all the rest of the year, suddenly a pile of pancakes looks like a better idea.

With brunch, a two-in-one meal of breakfast and lunch dishes, we have another chance to branch out a little, with prepare-ahead casseroles and fruit salads.

In the following pages, we'll start with simple breakfasts and gradually work towards more complex ones. I hope you'll find an appealing enough recipe or two to jolt you out of your routine.

OATMEAL PORRIDGE

Good news. Oatmeal does not have to be gluey! Lots of people can't stand sticky oatmeal. It suffers a little from a bad reputation, caused mostly, I'll bet, by sometimes artificially-flavored, pre-sweetened, powdery fluff in an envelope that turns to sludge when added to water and microwaved. Even quick-cooking oatmeal ends up too gummy for many people.

For non-sticky oatmeal, be sure to use old-fashioned rolled oats or steel cut oats and cook it as you might cook rice. Enhance your oatmeal with raisins, cinnamon, dried blueberries, dried apple, and dried cranberries. Top it with nuts, seeds, or fruit. Offer honey, sugar, white or brown, or even jam, to sweeten. Some will prefer it with milk or half-and-half or yogurt. Some like it with a dab of butter, sugar, and milk. Plus, oatmeal is economical. If you can wean porridge-haters off costly, sugary boxed cereal, you can save yourself a few dollars.

1 CUP WATER

¾ CUP NON-INSTANT ROLLED OATS

A FEW GRAINS OF SALT

Bring the water to a boil, then add the oatmeal and salt, and reduce the heat to simmer. Put a lid on the pan, slightly cocked to allow some steam to escape. Check the pan in ten minutes, and gently stir the oatmeal. Sample a few grains; if it is still a little dry, take off the heat, add a tablespoon or so of hot water, and put the lid on tightly. Let stand for three minutes, and sample again. Repeat if necessary. Oatmeal is done when the grains are puffed and tender and somewhat separate from one another. {Serves 2}

. . .

PAM'S ENHANCED OATMEAL PORRIDGE

Pam Chase reported that she and her husband, Lloyd, are oatmeal fans and sent her recipe, below, for a banana or apple version, which calls for vanilla or maple extract. "The extract makes a big difference," she said, and added, "Honey or maple

{ADVICE}

>> Consider soaking the oats overnight to hasten cooking next morning; then cook your oatmeal on top of the stove where you can watch it carefully; you may find you can eat in fifteen minutes from starting.

Use a higher proportion of oatmeal to water than is usually recommended on the package, bring the water to a boil before adding the oatmeal and setting a lid on the pot so it both simmers and steams a little.

For firm oatmeal, avoid vigorous stirring which breaks up the oat flakes; instead move the oatmeal gently with a spoon.

For softer porridge, add more water to the pan, up to twice as much water and oatmeal; stir it more often until you get a soft, sauce-like consistency.

Besides reheating it, you can treat leftover porridge like polenta. Slice it when it is cold, dip it in egg and flour or cornmeal, and fry it golden brown on both sides in oil or butter.

The Oatmeal Papers

*T*here are many oatmeal eaters among you. Some sit down cheerfully to giant bowlfuls with a huge array of add-ons. Others eat their oatmeal dutifully but joylessly, as if oatmeal were a kind of culinary hair shirt tolerated in penance for the sins of ice cream and steak.

Lots of Taste Buds readers joined the oatmeal conversation. Sandra Dinsmore wrote, "I never knew it was possible to make unsticky oatmeal. I haven't tasted it since I was about seven." She could never manage the "slimy, sticky mess" her mother made. After trying the method for firm oatmeal, she and I had an exchange about whether or not to use a double boiler to prevent oatmeal sticking on the pan.

To loosen any sticking I notice, I add a splash of cold water to the oatmeal, let it settle a moment, then nudge the porridge off the bottom of the pan with a spoon. Of course, if you wait too long to do this, and the oatmeal really catches, then you will just have to soak the pan, and use a scrubber to get it off. Or use a double boiler.

Doris Plumer wrote, "On the subject of yummy oatmeal...add barley to the oats during cooking for extra chewiness." Good idea. What about adding left-over cooked grains like rice, or farro, or bulgur?

syrup can be substituted for the brown sugar. Raisins can be added as well. Lloyd likes raisins with the apple version."

When she makes the apple version, she said, "I core, peel, dice it, and cook in the microwave for a minute or two, depending on the power of the oven." When she uses a banana, she mashes it while the oatmeal cooks.

Pam microwave-cooks porridge, a handy option to stove top.

FOR EACH SERVING:

1 CUP OLD FASHIONED OATS

DASH OF SALT

2 TEASPOON BROWN SUGAR, OR TO TASTE

2 TABLESPOONS FINELY CHOPPED WALNUTS

⅔ CUP WATER, PLUS A TEASPOON OR SO MORE TO COMPENSATE
    FOR THE WALNUTS

1 TEASPOON MAPLE OR VANILLA EXTRACT

RAISINS, OPTIONAL

BANANA OR APPLE

Put the oats, salt, sugar, walnuts, water, and extract, and raisins, if you use them, in a microwave-safe bowl, large enough for the number of servings you are making. Stir just a bit, and cook in the microwave three or four minutes, depending on the power level you use. When the oatmeal is done, take out of the microwave, carefully, because the bowl will be hot. Stir and let set a minute. Add mashed banana or apple, and eat plain, or with milk or half-and-half.

EGGS

Eggs make a speedy cooked breakfast. Fried, scrambled, soft boiled on toast, or hard-boiled to go: most of us can do these without a recipe. There are egg breakfast possibilities, however, that might need a little more advice.

. . .

SAVORY BREAKFAST EGGS

The operating principle here is the combination of a fresh, fragrant herb, a little garlic or onion, and an agreeable cheese to sprinkle on the top.

Possibilities include a little bit of cilantro, a piece of hot chili pepper finely chopped and a grating of jack cheese, which might make it a Tex-Mex egg. Chervil or tarragon, plus minced shallots, and a bit of grated gruyere cheese might make you think of France or Switzerland.

A TABLESPOON OF BUTTER

A TABLESPOON OF OLIVE OIL

A FEW LEAVES OF BASIL OR OTHER FRESH HERB

A LITTLE MINCED GARLIC OR SHALLOTS OR PEPPER

2 EGGS

PARMESAN CHEESE OR CHEESE OF YOUR CHOICE

Melt the butter in a frying pan with the olive oil over a low heat. Lay the basil leaves in the pan, and add the minced garlic, heating them until you can smell them and the herbs are wilted. Break the eggs on top of the herbs, grate some parmesan on top, and put a lid on the pan. Cook over a low heat until the whites are set, and the yolk is as well done as you prefer. Alternatively, run the eggs under the broiler briefly to cook the eggs and melt the cheese. {Serves 1}

• • •

SHIRRED EGGS

Strictly speaking, shirred eggs are a form of baked eggs; the French call it *oeufs en cocotte*, or casserole, which you might use if you are preparing eggs for a crowd, though for one or two people, a custard cup in a pan of water on the stove top serves beautifully.

Shirring gives you a chance to add flavor with herbs, cheese, and plus salt and pepper. Use herbs of your choice, fresh when available

DAB OF BUTTER
1 TABLESPOON OF MILK OR CREAM
SALT AND PEPPER
HERB OF CHOICE, OPTIONAL
CHEESE OF CHOICE, GRATED OR CRUMBLED, OPTIONAL
1 EGG

Place a shallow pan on medium heat with water enough to come halfway up the sides of custard cups or ramekins. Put a dab of butter in each cup. When it melts, swirl the butter in the cup to coat the sides. Add the milk or cream and a sprinkle of salt and pepper. If you choose other seasonings and cheese, add them. Break an egg into the cup, and as the white begins to set, use the tip of a dinner knife to move the yolk to the center of the white. Cover the pan, and check back in four minutes. Watch closely to determine when the white has been cooked, and the yolk is as runny as you like. Remove the cup from the water, and use the knife to loosen the egg, which you can slide onto toast to serve.

Eggs Florentine Variations

When spinach abounds, wilt a huge pile of it in a sauté pan, drop eggs on it, then slap on a lid to steam the eggs. A shave of parmesan, some salt and pepper, and you have Eggs Florentine. Vary that by using chard. (Does that make Eggs Chardentine?)

With either spinach or chard, consider vegging it up with sautéed onions and peppers. Chard stems, separated from the leafy portion, are good chopped like celery and cooked briefly before you add other ingredients.

Consider beating the egg a bit and adding it to the sautéed vegetables. A few swishes with a fork and the eggs are done, and ready to eat.

EGGS AND CHARD

1 TO 2 CHARD LEAVES DEPENDING ON SIZE

1 TO 2 TEASPOONS OF OLIVE OIL

SMALL ONION (OPTIONAL)

HALF A FRYING PEPPER (OPTIONAL)

YOUR CHOICE OF BASIL, OREGANO, PARSLEY, GARLIC TO TASTE

1 TO 2 EGGS PER PERSON

Strip the green portion of the chard off the stalk, and shred. Set aside. Chop the stalk into small pieces. Heat the oil in a sauté pan or use a non-stick pan and add the onion, pepper, and garlic, if you use them, and cook for two minutes or so over a medium heat, just until they begin to soften. Add the chard stems, and cook them for a minute or two, then add the shredded leaves. When the leaves have just wilted, add the eggs whole on top, cover with a lid to steam, and allow them to set until they are as well-done as you like. Alternatively, beat the eggs and pour them into the cooked vegetables, stirring once or twice until they are set. {*Makes a variable number of servings*}

· · ·
Eggs in a Nest

This lovely eggs-in-a-nest recipe came from Bobbie Lehigh in Eastport, whose daughter Kim Crabill of Portland, rediscovered in one of Bobbie's cookbooks, a *1994 Hometown Collection American's Best Recipes*. And their tinkerability quotient is pretty high, too.

(The recipe originally came from one Helen C. Felton who entered the recipe in a cookbook called *Cooking with Grace*, a community cookbook assembled for Grace Church School Parents' Association in New York City. Now you just never know, do you, where your recipe might end up when you offer it to a community organization for their fundraiser.)

Bobbie described Kim as gleeful with her success with the eggs, and surmised some of you readers could stand a little glee, too, as she said, "In these very difficult to watch days." I'll say.

Separate the eggs, beat the whites into stiff peaks for a meringue to spread on a slice of bread. Make a dent deep enough in the meringue to cradle the yolk, and then bake it. Bobbie wrote, "Kim and I thought a thin piece of ham, or bacon (cooled and cut up) or a slice of cheese would be nice added to the bread before the meringue is put on the bread, or/and an herb added to the meringue. Anyway, see what you can do with it."

1 SLICE OF BREAD

SUFFICIENT BUTTER TO SPREAD ON THE BREAD

1 LARGE EGG, SEPARATED

SALT AND PEPPER, SPRINKLE OF EACH

OPTIONAL ADD-INS: SLICED HAM, SALMON, HERBS, CHEESE

Heat the oven to 350 degrees. Put the bread on an ungreased baking sheet and spread with butter to taste on one side only. If you choose optional add-ins, add them to the bread now. Beat the egg white with any herbs or spices you desire until it forms stiff peaks Spread the meringue over the bread, and make a shallow dent in it with the back of a spoon. Gently slide the egg yolk into the dent. Bake for fifteen minutes for a still-soft yolk or add two more minutes if you prefer a firm yolk. Sprinkle with salt and pepper to serve. *{Serves 1}*

...

Egg Bakes or Breakfast Soufflés

This recipe comes from the menu of a bed and breakfast inn where I worked years ago. The family who ran the inn called them egg bakes, and often served them for family holiday breakfasts. At the inn, though, they thought that "egg bakes" wasn't quite the image they wanted to project so they grandly renamed them as breakfast soufflés.

They do puff up beautifully while baking, then instantly collapse when they come out of the oven.

Use glass custard cups if you have them or ramekins and plan to let them stand in the fridge overnight or at least for a few hours before baking.

> 1 SLICE OF SEMI-FIRM BREAD
> 1 TABLESPOON OF COOKED BREAKFAST SAUSAGE OR BACON CRUMBLED, OR CHOPPED HAM
> 1 TO 2 TABLESPOONS SHREDDED CHEDDAR OR JACK CHEESE
> ½ CUP MILK
> 1 SMALL EGG

Lightly grease the inside of your custard cup with butter, and press the bread into the cup, trimming excess off the top of the cup rim. Add your choice of meat to the cup; top it with the shredded cheese. Beat together the egg and milk and pour it over the meat and cheese until it shows through. It may soak up a little and need just topping off. Cover and put into the fridge overnight or for a few hours. When you are ready to bake them, heat the oven to 350 degrees. Put the cups into a shallow baking pan or on a baking sheet in case they bubble over. Bake for forty to forty-five minutes until puffed and golden brown on top. Serve immediately. {Serves 1}

PANCAKES AND FRENCH TOAST

Are you in a pancake rut? Happens easily if you have a favorite mix; it's just as easy to get out of by switching in a few other ingredients.

Oatmeal Cookie Pancakes: Omit half a cup of mix or flour if you bake from scratch and use a half cup of rolled oats, a handful of raisins, and a sprinkle of cinnamon, and proceed as usual.

Cornmeal and Corn Pancakes: Omit half a cup of mix or flour as above; add half cup of cornmeal, a quarter cup of corn kernels, and a shake of black pepper; then proceed as usual.

Apple Pancakes: Corn an apple and slice it about a quarter of an inch thick. Lay the slices on the griddle and cover with regular pancake batter, and cook as usual until you see bubbles on the pancake's surface, then flip the pancakes over.

• • •

SAVORY BACON, CHEDDAR, AND ONION PANCAKES

Substantial and delicious, pancakes like this make a wonderful weekend breakfast, even brunch. In a recipe like this, if it smells like onion, I figure it is fair game to use: leeks, scallions, a big bunch of chives, or just plain finely chopped onions will all work.

2 CUPS ALL-PURPOSE FLOUR

1½ TEASPOONS BAKING POWDER

½ TEASPOON BAKING SODA

1 CUP SHREDDED CHEDDAR

1 SMALL ONION FINELY CHOPPED OR 4 SCALLIONS SLICED THINLY

3 OR 4 STRIPS COOKED BACON, CRUMBLED OR CHOPPED

2 LARGE EGGS

1½ CUPS MILK

2 TABLESPOONS VEGETABLE OIL

EXTRA BACON FOR GARNISH, OPTIONAL

{ADVICE}

« If you make your pancakes from scratch, mix all the dry ingredients together ahead of time, and store in a container until you are ready to make the pancakes. Similarly, providing you'll make the pancakes in a day or so, you can also whisk together the eggs, milk, and oil and refrigerate in a jar until you are ready to mix them into the dry ingredients.

Sift or whisk together flour, sugar, baking powder, and baking soda. Mix shredded cheddar, bacon, and onions into the dry ingredients. Whisk together eggs, milk, and oil and add them to the flour mixture with a few swift strokes just to moisten the mixture. Cook on a medium hot skillet until the edges are firm and the bottom of the pancakes are golden; turn them over for a few moments to finish cooking. Serve with maple syrup. {*Serves 4*}

• • •

FRENCH TOAST

French toast is actually a fried form of bread pudding. The outside ought to be a little crisp and the center ought to be soft and pudding-like, but not mushy.

You can vary French toast just by using different kinds of bread, preferably the sort that gets a little stale like homemade or artisanal breads, or sweet breads like challah, raisin bread, or brioche, though to be truthful, I've used fresh bread and it worked just fine.

You can also vary French toast by using different kinds of milk—cow, almond, coconut, buttermilk, lactose-free, half-and-half, cream, evaporated—and just by using eggs alone. Years ago, I worked, at a bed and breakfast inn on Islesboro, with a wonderful Jamaican cook, Kerene Spence who always added a splash or two of orange juice to her French toast mixture. You might like sweetening the egg and milk mixture with either white or brown sugar, honey, or maple syrup.

¼ TO ⅓ CUP MILK

1 LARGE EGG

1 TEASPOON SUGAR (OPTIONAL, MORE TO TASTE)

A SPRINKLE OF GRATED NUTMEG

2 TO 3 SLICES OF DAY OLD BREAD

OIL OR BACON FAT

Whisk together milk, egg, sugar, if using it, and nutmeg, and pour into a shallow bowl pan, like a pie plate or cake pan. Lay the bread in the mixture and allow it to soak up enough to soften bread, turning bread at least once. Heat a fry pan until a drop of water will bounce when dripped on it. Oil or grease lightly. Fry the soaked bread until it is quite golden brown; then turn and brown the other side. Keep it warm in the oven at a low temperature until you are ready to serve it.

MUFFINS

...

Blueberry Muffins

Along with lobster, visitors to Maine hope to score some blue-berries and a muffin, well-studded with them, is one way to go.

Elaine Lowell of Prospect Harbor sent along this charming recipe along with the recommendation to sprinkle sugar on top to give them a little crunch, adding berries to the flour mixture *before* adding the milk, oil, and egg. She advised, "Stir gently with a fork, just until dry ingredients are moistened. Batter will be lumpy." It will be, and the muffins come out beautifully.

ELAINE LOWELL'S BLUEBERRY MUFFINS

2 CUPS FLOUR

½ CUP SUGAR

3 TEASPOONS BAKING POWDER

½ TEASPOON SALT

1 CUP FRESH BLUEBERRIES

1 CUP MILK

⅓ CUP VEGETABLE OIL OR MELTED BUTTER

1 EGG, SLIGHTLY BEATEN

SUGAR FOR SPRINKLING, IF DESIRED

Preheat the oven to 400 degrees. Grease muffin tins, or line with paper baking cups. In a large bowl, whisk together the flour, sugar, and baking powder. Stir the blueberries into the flour mixture. Combine milk, oil, and egg and beat with a fork to mix. Make a well in the flour mixture, and pour the milk mixture into it all at once. Stir gently with a fork or spoon just until the dry ingredients are all moistened. Distribute batter among the muffin cups and sprinkle the tops lightly with sugar if desired. Bake for 20 to 25 minutes until golden brown and a tester inserted comes out clean. {*Makes a dozen to eighteen, depending on the size of your muffin tins*}

. . .

BRAN AND OATMEAL MUFFINS

Bran has such a dowdy reputation, though lots of us are grateful for its beneficial effect on something my mother used to call, euphemistically, "what ails you." Bran–intensive cereal, the most obvious one being All–Bran, which occupies a very small space on grocery shelves and looks like an unappetizing pile of twigs when turned out of the box. My island friend and neighbor Derreth Roberts makes the twigs into muffins and stashes a batch of them in the fridge or freezer, to eat for breakfast along with fruit and yogurt. Wicked wholesome what with bran, oats, and molasses. Raisins are optional.

You don't need cup papers. Just grease your muffin pan well. These mix up very quickly once the bran and oatmeal is soaked in the milk, a perfect project for a weekend breakfast or brunch.

1 CUP ALL-BRAN CEREAL

1 CUP ROLLED OATS

1½ CUP MILK

1 EGG

1 CUP FLOUR

½ BAKING SODA

½ CUP MOLASSES

½ CUP OF RAISINS (OPTIONAL)

Set the All-Bran and rolled oats to soak in the milk to soften for about fifteen minutes. Heat the oven to 350 and generously grease your muffin tins. Mix the egg, flour and baking soda into the soaked bran and oatmeal, and stir it well. Then add the molasses and optional raisins, and mix well. Spoon the batter into the muffin pan. Bake for fifteen to twenty minutes. When done the muffin tops will be puffed, firm, and dry and a tester inserted comes out clean. Remove from the oven and let cool before removing the muffins from the pan. {*Makes about a dozen muffins*}

BREAKFAST HASHES, FRITTATA, AND STRATAS

Now we are firmly into cooked breakfasts that require time to prepare, great for weekends, brunches, and social gatherings.

. . .

Corned Beef Hash

In New England, leftover boiled dinner with its corned beef and cabbage, potatoes, and carrots, and sometimes onions, ought to turn up the next day as hash. You can make sure there are leftovers by cooking a few extra potatoes to go with the ample quantity of meat. Because they promote sogginess, you might omit cabbage or onions and use freshly chopped onion instead.

The proportion of meat to vegetables ought to suit your personal taste. If you want what is known as red flannel hash, you have to add cooked beets which usually turn everything a lurid pink.

Usually, corned beef has enough fat in it that no extra is need to crisp it up on a frying pan, but a dribble of vegetable oil could help if the hash sticks. Serve with an egg on top if you want a more robust serving.

BOILED CORNED BEEF

BOILED POTATOES

BOILED CARROTS

BOILED BEETS (OPTIONAL)

1 SMALL ONION, CHOPPED

VEGETABLE OIL OR DRIPPINGS

Coarsely chop the beef, potatoes, carrots, and optional onions into your preferred fineness of texture. Fold in the onions and turn onto a frying pan at medium high heat. Brown hash, adding a little oil or drippings as needed.

{ADVICE}

When chopping corn beef (or roast beef) for hash, out comes the old family chopping bowl and the chopping knife with the curved blade and wooden handle on top. I dump the ingredients in it, and chop them all up. If you are a masterful pulser with a food processor, you could get away with chopping in that, but I find that the machine is usually too powerful to trust my meat and vegetables to it. You can, of course, also chop on a cutting board with a chef's knife, rocking the blade down through the potatoes, meat, bits of carrots, or other vegetables.

Variable Frittata

Frittatas transform bits and pieces into a flavorful whole. They handily absorb leftover cooked vegetables like broccoli, cauliflower, peas, corn, potatoes, as well as well a handful of fresh ones like chard, kale, spinach, and bok choy. Little bits of meat too small to make a meal out of or a couple of ounces of sausage, bacon, smoked fish, ham, or cooked poultry. A little chopped onion, minced garlic, or herbs to season it, add eggs and you have a meal.

With the recipe below, you can easily convert the frittata into a vegetarian one by simply omitting the meat.

2 STRIPS OF BACON OR 2 OUNCES SAUSAGE

OLIVE OIL

1 SMALL ONION, A SHALLOT, OR 1 LEEK CHOPPED

HANDFUL OF SPINACH, OR CHARD, SHREDDED

1 EGG PER PERSON PLUS 1 FOR THE PAN, BEATEN

SALT AND PEPPER TO TASTE

CHEESE (CHEDDAR, SWISS, JACK, MOZZARELLA) SHREDDED

Fry the sausage, bacon, or ham until it is crisp. Set aside to drain. If there is not enough grease in the pan to cook the onion in, add oil and onion, and cook it until it's softened. Add the spinach or chard; stir gently until they wilt. Pour the beaten eggs over the ingredients in the pan, shaking the pan a little to distribute the eggs. Set the heat to a medium-low and put a lid on the pan. When the eggs are barely set, sprinkle the cheese on top, replace the lid, and allow the cheese to melt and the eggs to finish cooking. Serve.

Stratas

*L*ayers of bread, eggs, meat or shellfish, and cheese baked in a casserole can often be assembled in advance, and held for a few hours in the fridge, even overnight, to bake in the morning for brunch. A simple combination feeds a family and dressed up a little serves company with fruit salad and sweet bread on the side. OJ to drink; or how about mimosas? Make sure there is coffee, too, or tea.

• • •

CRAB STRATA

Caroline Rittenhouse from Deer Isle, who got it from the Stonington artist Michie Stovall O'Day, sent this recipe along. Caroline and Michie like to use leftover baguettes for the bread, and you can use that, too, or any good firm bread, as long as it is not so assertively flavored that it diminishes the crab. Whether or not you take the crusts off or not is up to you.

If you are one of those patient folks who like to pick crab and have access to some, then you can save a few dollars, otherwise spring for a pint container. You can also use lobster and mix it with the crab; or go with either alone.

4 TO 6 SLICES OF BREAD, OR AS NEEDED

8 OUNCES OF SHREDDED CHEDDAR, MILD OR SHARP ACCORDING
    TO TASTE

16 OUNCES OF CRAB MEAT

4 TABLESPOONS OF BUTTER, MELTED

3 EGGS BEATEN

1 PINT HALF-AND-HALF, OR LIGHT CREAM

½ TEASPOON DRY MUSTARD

¼ TEASPOON CRUSHED RED PEPPER OR HOT SAUCE TO TASTE

SALT AND PEPPER TO TASTE

Grease a nine-by-thirteen-inch glass or ceramic casserole dish. Lay the bread in bottom of the casserole. Sprinkle two-thirds of the cheese over it, then the crab, and dribble with the butter. Beat together the eggs, half-and-half, and seasonings and pour that over the layers in the casserole. Top with the remaining cheese. Cover and refrigerate overnight or four to six hours. When you are ready to bake it, heat the oven to 350, and bake the casserole for about an hour, uncovered, until it is puffy and golden. *{Serves 8 to 10}*

. . .

FARMER'S BREAKFAST

Breakfast for one or more, this breakfast is highly expandable and flexible enough to allow for meat variations, though the classic is sausage, either links that you cut into small pieces or bulk sausage crumbled up. Vary your cheese selection, using Swiss, cheddar, or smoked cheese.

YOUR CHOICE OF BREAKFAST MEAT: SAUSAGE, LINK OR BULK
COOKED POTATOES
ONIONS
EGGS, BEATEN
CHEESE, GRATED
OPTIONAL ADD-INS: PEPPERS, GARLIC, MUSHROOMS
SALT AND PEPPER TO TASTE

Cook the breakfast meat on a frying pan. Drain off excess fat. Add the potatoes, onions, optional add-ins, and cook until the potatoes are browned and onions are softened. Pour the beaten eggs over the ingredients on the fry pan. Add salt and pepper. Allow the eggs to cook and thicken, turn once, and when they are firm, top with the grated cheese. Run under a broiler briefly if you wish.

. . .

SPINACH OR KALE, EGG, CHEESE, AND HAM ON ENGLISH MUFFIN

OLIVE OIL
SMALL PIECE OF ONION OR SHALLOT, MINCED
A HANDFUL OF SHREDDED SPINACH OR KALE LEAVES

1 OR 2 THIN SLICES OF HAM ABOUT THE SIZE OF AN ENGLISH MUFFIN

1 ENGLISH MUFFIN

1 OR 2 EGGS

1 OR 2 THIN SLICES OF CHEDDAR CHEESE

Put a little oil in a sauté pan, add the minced shallot or onion, and heat until you can smell the onion cooking. Add the spinach or kale and cook only until it is wilted. Take off the heat. Warm the ham on a fry pan or griddle and toast the English muffin. Lay the spinach or kale on the muffin, and top with the ham. Fry the egg(s), turning once, then lay it/them on top of the ham, and a thin slice of cheddar on top of that. Serve right away. *{Serves 1}*

· · ·

Sausage Stuffed Baked Apple

This recipe was inspired by a breakfast I like very much: slices of apples sauteed next to a link or two of sausage eaten hot off the pan.

1 APPLE PER PERSON

A LARGE SPOONFUL, ABOUT 1½ TABLESPOONS OF BULK

    BREAKFAST SAUSAGE, PER PERSON

A TINY BIT OF ONION, 1 TEASPOON OR LESS, PER APPLE

Heat the oven to 350 degrees. Core the apples, and place in baking pan. Mix together the sausage and onion. Cram each apple with sausage using your thumb to push it into the core. Spread a little extra sausage, if you have it, over the top of the apple. Bake for thirty-five to forty-five minutes or until the apple bursts open and the sausage on top is browned. *{Makes as many servings as you have apples}*

{ADVICE}

« *Here's apple coring advice. Avoid using a straight tube apple corer that whizzes through the apple, making a hole in the bottom while missing some seeds and the tough little curved lining to the seed case. Get out your trusty melon baller, use the small end, and dig in at the stem end until you can see the star shape holding the seeds, and scoop out all the seeds. Then stop.*

ONE LIQUID
BREAKFAST

. . .

Kale Shake

½ PEELED, FROZEN BANANA
½ PEAR OR APPLE
1½ CUPS OF KALE, SHREDDED AND TIGHTLY PACKED
1 CUP SOY MILK
½ TEASPOON GINGER

Put everything into a blender and liquefy it. {*Serves 1*}

5

A Mountain of Desserts

Out of the fifty United States, only fourteen have official state desserts or pies. These designations are usually made by a resolution of the state legislature and it must make for a light-hearted debate as elected officials discuss and vote on how their state distinguishes itself at the end of meal or next to the cash register at convenience stores.

Maine's official sweet tooth chose Whoopie Pies as our official state "treat," and blueberry pie, only if made with Maine blueberries, as our official state pie.

These two barely scratch the surface of the desserts Maine people relish. Here are cakes, including some made with vegetables, plus cookies, pies and galettes, fruity desserts and frozen ones.

CAKES

. . .

One, Two, Three, Four Coconut Cake

A passing reference in Taste Buds about Coconut Cake resulted in a flurry of requests for the recipe. Sandi Rowe Umble in Holden wrote, "My mouth was watering when you talked about the one, two, three, four coconut cake!" Tim Burleigh in Dover-Foxcroft wanted the recipe as did Michaeleen Ward who remembered that her mother made coconut cakes. "But I never asked for the recipe. Hindsight is always so good," she observed. And then it turned out that Arline Deshane in Enfield wanted to make coconut cake for her granddaughter's June birthday.

The recipe is a personal favorite of mine which I discovered years ago in a sea captain's wife's manuscript recipe book from around 1880. I even made it from fresh coconut that I grated by hand. If you have even a modicum of purist in you, try doing that sometime. The result is unbelievably fabulous, delicious and rich, and despite your skinned and raw knuckles, you will be glad.

You can use unsweetened grated coconut, freshen it somewhat by tossing it with a little cream dribbled into it, enough to moisten it slightly and restore the needed oiliness. Only use sweetened coconut if you like very sweet cake.

Frost this as you wish. Seven Minute Boiling Icing works; you can split each layer to create four layers and put icing or filling between each by using more frosting, or jam or jelly in between layers.

4 CUPS FLOUR

1 TEASPOON CREAM OF TARTAR

½ TEASPOON BAKING SODA

1 CUP (OR 2 STICKS) BUTTER

2 CUPS SUGAR

1 CUP MILK

2½ CUPS GRATED COCONUT

3 EGG WHITES

Heat the oven to 350 degrees. Grease and flour two nine-inch diameter cake pans, two inches deep, or line them with parchment paper. Sift together the dry ingredients. Cream together the butter and sugar. Beat the egg whites until they form stiff peaks. Add the dry ingredients alternately with the milk. Beat in the coconut. Stir into the batter about one-fourth of the beaten whites, then fold in the remaining whites. The batter will be fairly firm. Spread it evenly in the pans. Bake for forty-five minutes or until a tester inserted comes out clean, and the cake surface is golden. Allow to cool, then turn out of the pans and let cool before icing. {Makes a 9 inch cake}

One, Two, Three, Four

*T*he number-filled name of the cake comes from a very old mnemonic device to remind the baker to use one cup of butter, two cups of sugar, three eggs, and four cups of flour.

Similarly, pound cake gets its name from the recipe's requirement of one pound each of butter, sugar, flour, and eggs.

. . .

GOLD CAKE

A hundred and fifty years ago or so, Gold Cakes always accompanied Silver Cakes in cookbooks because the Silver Cakes, like the Coconut one, use only beaten whites. The Coconut Cake above will leave you with three yolks to use up plus others if you make boiled icing. The 1917 copy of *Mrs. Allen's Cookbook*, by Ida Bailey Allen includes a recipe for Gold Cake calling for four yolks plus one whole egg. You could probably get away with three yolks and one whole egg. Or add one more egg white to the coconut cake.

Mrs. Allen also recommends, "Frost with chocolate icing," a very good idea.

½ CUP (1 STICK) BUTTER

1 CUP SUGAR

1 EGG

4 EGG YOLKS

1 TEASPOON VANILLA

1¾ CUPS FLOUR

2 TEASPOONS BAKING POWDER

½ CUP MILK

Heat the oven to 350 degrees, and grease and flour a tube pan. Cream together the butter and sugar, add the whole egg, and then gradually the yolks, beating after each addition. Sift together the flour and baking powder, and add it alternately to the egg and sugar mixture with the milk. Pour batter into the tube pan and bake for forty minutes, or until it begins to pull away from the edges of the pan and is firm to the touch. {Makes a 10 inch cake}

. . .

Flourless Chocolate Cake

Smooth and creamy, like the silkiest fudge you ever ate, this flourless cake will satisfy your chocolate cravings. All eight inches of its diameter is so rich that no one can eat a huge slab of it. Plus, it really needs a counterpoint of sour flavor to take the edge off the sweet unctuousness. The blood orange syrup and fruit suggested below does the job.

The recipe comes from my island neighbor and friend Kathy Kerr whose brings it to potlucks. You don't have to be avoiding gluten to appreciate a flourless dessert.

The cake's center puffs up nicely though the cake settles a bit when it cools.

You can spread a glaze of chocolate ganache over it.

FOR THE CAKE:

1 CUP SEMISWEET OR BITTERSWEET CHOCOLATE CHIPS

8 TABLESPOONS (OR 1 STICK) BUTTER

¾ CUP GRANULATED SUGAR

¼ TEASPOON SALT

1 TO 2 TEASPOONS ESPRESSO POWDER, OPTIONAL

1 TEASPOON VANILLA EXTRACT

3 LARGE EGGS

½ CUP DUTCH-PROCESS COCOA

{ADVICE}

» Use the best chocolate chips you can afford. As reformulated products emerge, you'll find that some of the standard brands produce chips that don't melt out smoothly. That might be acceptable for cookies, but for pudding, sauces, or a cake like this, that doesn't work.

The recipe also calls for espresso coffee powder. One teaspoon, says King Arthur, enhances the flavor while two teaspoons gives the cake a mocha flavor. If you don't customarily keep espresso powder on hand, substitute instant coffee.

Heat the oven to 375 degrees. Lightly grease an eight-inch pan and line the bottom with parchment paper, also greased. Put the butter and chocolate in a heat proof bowl and warm in a microwave or over boiling water until the butter is melted, and the chips soften. Stir until the chips melt completely and put the mixture into a medium mixing bowl. Stir in the sugar, salt, espresso powder, and vanilla. Add the eggs one at a time, beating after each until the batter is smooth. Add the cocoa powder and mix just enough to combine. The batter will be a bit firm. Spread in the pan. Bake for twenty-five minutes, then check to see if the center is puffed and a tester comes out clean, adding time until you achieve that. Remove and let cool for five minutes. Loosen the edge of the cake with a knife, run around the perimeter and put a plate over the pan and turn the cake out. Let cool completely.

FOR THE GLAZE:
  ½ CUP SEMISWEET OR BITTERSWEET CHOCOLATE CHIPS
  ¼ CUP HEAVY CREAM

In a heatproof bowl, or in a small pan in hot water, heat the cream until hot but not simmering. Stir in the chocolate chips to combine, then rest for about five minutes, and stir until smooth, reheating if necessary. Spread over the cooled cake, allowing the glaze to dribble down the sides of the cake.

• • •

BLOOD ORANGE SYRUP AND CANDIED SLICES

With dark purple interiors and purple streaked orange rinds, blood oranges are a tad sour, not as sweet as their all-orange counterparts. Make a syrup with the juice and zest of two blood oranges. Slice a third orange as thinly as you can and simmer the slices in some of the syrup until they candy and the rinds become translucent. The candied rind makes a great garnish and serve the cake on a plate flooded with the syrup.

JUICE AND RIND OF 2 BLOOD ORANGES

WATER

1 CUP GRANULATED SUGAR

1 WHOLE BLOOD ORANGE, SLICED THINLY

Put the juice and rind of the blood orange into a measuring cup and top it off with water until it measures one cup. Combine the water and juice with one cup of granulated sugar and bring to a boil until sugar is entirely dissolved to make syrup. Cool before using. If you wish to candy orange slices, put the sliced orange in a shallow pan and pour syrup over it until they are barely covered. Simmer until the rinds become translucent. Lift the slices out and cool.

Cake and Emancipation

On April 16, lots of us celebrate finishing our income taxes but the more significant thing to observe is Emancipation Day. President Abraham Lincoln signed the act on April 16, 1862, which immediately freed all the slaves in Washington, D.C. These days, April 16 is an official holiday in D.C. It took until the end of the Civil War in 1865 for emancipation to take effect nationwide.

To raise money for the Anti-Slavery cause, a movement decades-old by the time Lincoln freed the slaves, Mary Merrick Brooks, an abolitionist in Concord, Massachusetts, used to make and sell this perfectly lovely tea cake.

Ruth Thurston in Machias sent me the recipe years ago, mostly, I suspect, because she knows I am intrigued by historical ones, and years of baking up treats from the 1800s has taught me that some of these old-fashioned things are a nice break from chocolate chip mania or trendy caramel and sea-salt.

...

Brooks Cake

This nineteenth-century tea cake made with real butter, plus flour, sugar, eggs, and milk, studded with currants, is easy to assemble and delicious. It will remind you of a pound cake, similar in flavor and in its dense, moist texture. It will tolerate a ride in a lunch bag to school or office, can be toasted lightly, and is delicious warm with a bit of butter spread on it.

The recipe is easily doubled, make one to eat now and to share or freeze. If you use a mixer, which poor Mrs. Brooks didn't have, the assembly is speedy.

½ CUP OR 1 STICK OF BUTTER

1 CUP SUGAR

2 EGGS

2 CUPS FLOUR

½ TEASPOON BAKING POWDER

½ CUP MILK

1 CUP OR FOUR OUNCES DRIED CURRANTS PLUMPED IN A
    LITTLE HOT WATER

Heat an oven to 350 degrees. Grease a nine-by-five-inch loaf pan or line it with parchment paper. Cream together butter and sugar. Beat in the eggs one at a time. Whisk together the flour and baking powder. Add the flour mixture and the milk alternately to the butter, sugar, and egg mixture, beating the batter on a low speed until it is all incorporated. Drain and fold in the currants. Bake for fifty to sixty minutes or until a tester inserted comes out clean. The loaf may crack on the top and ought to have a pale golden color. {Makes a 9½ inch cake}

Vegetables in Funny Places

We usually eat our vegetables as entrees or side dishes. Over the years, readers have sent recipes for vegetables in our desserts, usually in cake, which is kind of a funny place for a vegetable. *Maine Home Cooking*, published in 2012, featured a spectacular chocolate cake loaded up with zucchini. Here are four more vegetable-laden cakes.

. . .

Pumpkin Spice Cake

{ADVICE}

>> *One fresh pie pumpkin ought to make one pie. When cooked it may produce about two cups of pureed pulp, but if you end up with a little less, you'll approximate a standard fifteen-ounce can of prepared pumpkin. A couple of tablespoons one way or another makes so little difference that you needn't worry about it*

We eat pumpkin in pie or sweet bread so often that it's hard to remember that pumpkin is a vegetable. Pumpkin isn't just for pie. The spices in this cake distinguish it from pumpkin bread. Consider frosting it with good old cream cheese frosting.

2 CUPS FLOUR

2 TEASPOONS BAKING POWDER

2 TEASPOONS BAKING SODA

1 TEASPOON SALT

1½ TEASPOONS CINNAMON

1 TEASPOON GINGER

½ TEASPOON NUTMEG

¼ TEASPOON CLOVES

¼ CUP OR ONE-HALF STICK BUTTER

½ CUP GRANULATED SUGAR

½ CUP, TIGHTLY PACKED, DARK BROWN SUGAR

½ CUP VEGETABLE OIL

3 EGGS

1½ TO 1¾ CUPS PUMPKIN PUREE

⅓ CUP WATER

Heat the oven to 350 degrees and grease and flour a nine-by-thirteen-inch baking pan or line with parchment paper. Sift together flour, baking powder and soda, salt, and the spices.

Cream together butter and granulated and brown sugars. Add and beat in oil and eggs. Mix in pumpkin. Add the dry ingredients alternately with the buttermilk and mix enough to make a smooth batter. Pour into the baking pan and bake for thirty to thirty-five minutes or until a tester inserted comes out clean. For serving, dust with confectioner's sugar, or sprinkle with cinnamon sugar, or frost with your favorite cream cheese frosting. {Makes a 9 x 13 cake}

. . .

Sweet Potato Cake

Another offering from Ruth Thurston in Machias will remind you of carrot cakes, pumpkin cakes, and squash cakes. So, probably the moral of the story is if you have a hard yellow or orange vegetable you don't know what else to do with, use it to make cake.

This one has a lot of flavor and character; spicy, moist, and firm with a charming crusty exterior when fresh from the oven. Oil as the main shortening promotes a lovely texture.

Feel free to increase the amount of spice to taste.

Frost it or not; plain confectioners' sugar sprinkled over top will do just fine or serve it with whipped cream. The cake is large. Bake it in a Bundt or tube pan.

2 CUPS ALL-PURPOSE FLOUR

2 TEASPOONS BAKING SODA

2 TEASPOONS BAKING POWDER

2 TEASPOONS GROUND CINNAMON

1 TEASPOON GINGER

½ TEASPOON ALLSPICE OR CLOVES

½ TEASPOON SALT

2 CUPS SUGAR

4 EGGS

1 CUP VEGETABLE OIL

1 POUND OR 2 CUPS COOKED SWEET POTATO

1 CUP CHOPPED NUTS, PECAN OR WALNUTS, OPTIONAL

Heat the oven to 350 degrees. Oil a tube or Bundt pan and flour it. Sift together the flour, baking soda and powder, and spices and salt, then set aside. Beat together sugar, eggs, oil, and sweet potato until very well blended. Add the sifted dry ingredients and beat for a couple minutes. Fold in the optional nuts. Pour batter into the baking pan and bake for an hour and test to see if a tester inserted comes out clean, and the cake has pulled from the edges of the pan; if necessary, bake for up to ten minutes more. Release from the pan and cool.

. . .

Parsnip Cake with Cream Cheese Frosting

Not everybody likes parsnips but they will like this parsnip cake. It's likely that the idea for this recipe originally came from carrot cake—they're both grate-able, sweet roots. If you have a favorite carrot cake recipe, you could, in fact, use parsnips in place of the carrots.

CAKE:

2 CUPS FLOUR

1 TEASPOON BAKING POWDER

1 TEASPOON BAKING SODA

2 TEASPOONS CINNAMON

¼ TEASPOON SALT

½ CUP BUTTER

½ CUT VEGETABLE OIL

¾ CUP LIGHT BROWN SUGAR

¾ CUP SUGAR

4 EGGS

2½ CUPS SHREDDED PARSNIPS (3 AVERAGE SIZED PARSNIPS)

¾ CUP WALNUTS GROUND

1 TEASPOON VANILLA

MILK

Heat the oven to 350. Grease and flour a tube pan. Sift the dry ingredients together and set aside. Beat together the butter, oil, and sugars. Add the eggs one at a time, beat well after each. Gradually add the dry ingredients, beating, and then add the parsnips, nuts, and vanilla. If the batter is stiff dribble in a little milk until the batter is soft enough to drop. Spread in the pan.

Bake for forty minutes or until a tester inserted comes out clean. Allow to cool before frosting. Any of the cakes with vegetables in them benefit from frosting made with cream cheese.

CREAM CHEESE FROSTING:
- ¼ CUP BUTTER, SOFTENED
- 4 OUNCES OF CREAM CHEESE
- 2 CUPS OF CONFECTIONERY SUGAR
- 1 TEASPOON VANILLA

Beat all together until smooth enough to spread. *{Yields enough for 12-18 servings}*

⇛ COOKIES AND BARS ⇚

. . .

CHOCOLATE CHIP OATMEAL COOKIES

Ben and Carrie Yardley in Yarmouth provided this recipe for a make-it-now, bake-it-later cookie.

- 1 CUP (2 STICKS) BUTTER
- 1 CUP LIGHT BROWN SUGAR
- 1 CUP GRANULATED SUGAR
- 2 EGGS
- 1 TEASPOON VANILLA
- 2⅓ CUPS FLOUR
- 1 TEASPOON BAKING SODA
- 1 TEASPOON SALT
- 2⅓ CUPS QUICK ROLLED OATS (OR 2 CUPS NON-INSTANT ROLLED OATS)
- 1 CUP SEMI-SWEET CHOCOLATE CHIPS

Soften the butter and cream well with the brown and white sugars; beat in the eggs and vanilla. Whisk or sift together the flour, baking soda, and salt, then add to the butter, egg, and sugar mixture. Fold in the oatmeal and chocolate chips. If you wish to refrigerate them, divide the dough into three parts,

» You can buy chocolate chip cookie dough in those plastic covered logs to slice off and bake whenever you want the house to fill up with sweet baking smells. Or you can mix this dough, roll it up in waxed paper or plastic wrap and stick it in the fridge to bake whenever you need cookies. The homemade ones are cheaper and don't have any creepy ingredients in them.

When you pull them out of the fridge to bake, the log will be very firm; use a very sharp and sturdy knife for slicing. Aim for cookies about three-eighths of an inch thick–that is, halfway between one quarter and one-half inch thick. A quarter of an inch is a tad too thin and half an inch a little too thick. Suit your-self. They don't spread very much at all.

form each part into a log shape and wrap in waxed paper or plastic wrap. Refrigerate for as much as a week. When you are ready to use them, preheat the oven to 375 degrees. Slice off the desired thickness and place on a greased baking sheet. Bake for about twelve to fourteen minutes or until light brown. {Makes 4 dozen three-inch cookies}

. . .

CLOVE COOKIES

Imagine gingersnaps seasoned instead with cloves, round and crinkled on top with a little sugar sprinkled on. For the holidays you could make it a fancy sugar like gold or big silvery crystals or even a holiday sprinkle of some sort.

Barbara Talamo, my island neighbor, introduced me to these tasty and flexible cookies. For example, you can vary the size. A walnut sized blob of dough makes larger cookies but fewer of them. Or take a spoon (like the ones you use at table) and scoop up enough to fill the end for smaller cookies. Flatten them a little to make it easier to decorate. Mix a little sugar and ground cloves together and sprinkle that on top before baking to boost the clove flavor.

    2¼ CUPS FLOUR
    ½ TEASPOON SALT
    1 TEASPOON BAKING SODA
    1 TABLESPOON GROUND CINNAMON
    2 TEASPOONS GROUND CLOVES
    1 CUP SUGAR
    ¾ CUP VEGETABLE OIL
    ¼ CUP MOLASSES
    1 EGG

Heat the oven to 350 and spread parchment paper on a couple of cookie sheets. Sift together the flour, salt, baking soda, cinnamon and cloves and set aside. Beat together the sugar, vegetable oil, and molasses until everything is completely incorporated. Beat in the egg. Add the flour mixture and beat until the dough is quite stiff, about two minutes with an electric beater. Drop balls of dough on your cookie sheets in whatever size you prefer, allowing them to spread at least two inches. Bake for about fourteen minutes, but check at twelve in case your oven is faster. The cookies will be brown, flat, and have crinkled texture. Cool and store in a tightly covered container. {Makes about 5 dozen two-inch cookies}

. . .

CREAM FILLED OATMEAL COOKIES

Ina Hollins in Northport tweaked this recipe somewhat in her making. For instance, she says that if you haven't got dark brown sugar, just use light, and add a little molasses. She really approves of cloves in it. Despite the instructions to use quick cooking oats, you can use standard rolled oats, pulsed a few times in the food processor. Lacking heavy cream, use half-and-half.

Ina pointed out that the cookies really spread so make them small or be sure to give them plenty of room to expand. Make sure you chill the dough. The original recipe calls for a whacking great three tablespoons of dough per cookie which makes a cream pie the size of the commercial original. You can make them smaller if you don't think you want that much dessert in one sitting.

1 CUP, OR 2 STICKS BUTTER

1 CUP DARK BROWN SUGAR

½ CUP GRANULATED SUGAR

1 EGG

2 TEASPOONS VANILLA

2 CUPS FLOUR

1 TEASPOON BAKING SODA

1 TEASPOON CINNAMON

¼ TEASPOON CLOVES

3 CUPS ROLLED OATS, PREFERABLY QUICK COOKING

Heat the oven to 375 degrees and line your cookie sheets with parchment paper or grease them very well. Cream together the butter and sugars until the mixture is light. Add the egg and vanilla and beat together. Whisk together the flour, baking soda, and spices then add the oats and mix to distribute the oats and flour together. Add to the butter and sugar mixture and be sure to gather up dry ingredients at the bottom of bowl. Place

« *TAKING IT A LITTLE EASY*
Sometimes if you have a slow moment or two, and you know you'll be busy in days ahead, measure out and stash the dry ingredients for cookies or cakes in a container. When you are ready to bake, just grab the mix and add it to the sugar, egg, and shortening mix

Or mix the cookies now and bake them later. Put the dough in a container in the fridge and bake off a panful just when you need a cookie. They'll taste better freshly baked than cookies baked ahead and frozen.

Little Debbie Knockoffs

Each summer Islesboro's library's friends group holds a book and bake sale. Not just cakes and cookies, breads and pies but jams, jellies, pickles and chutney are snapped up by summer and year-round residents alike. This summer, one of the delectables found its way post-sale to a potluck supper I attended where it was served for dessert: truly yummy, fat oatmeal cookies filled up with vanilla flavored frosting.

When I tracked down their maker, I discovered it was Ina Hollins, who lives in Northport and spends time on Islesboro in summer. She willingly shared the recipe which she originally found on the internet at *carlsbadcravings.com*.

That's when I learned that the recipe was intended to produce a homemade version of a popular commercial treat in the Little Debbie family. Those kinds of treats weren't ever part of my childhood though my mom bought Fig Newtons and Pecan Sandies and a few others. I may have lusted after factory-made pastries, but if my grandad gave me a dime, I always favored a Three Musketeers bar. Generally, little chocolate covered cupcakes with white squiggles on top, or gooey, cellophane-wrapped anythings were relegated to the category of throwing good money after bad. I recall thinking that probably the fruit-flavored, sugar syrup Zarex, was wonderful but mom and grandma, too, called it "belly wash" so that was that. Probably a good thing.

Nowadays, there is a whole species of recipe found online that replicates popular commercial dishes and products. While it's not exactly what you'd call health food, the following is a perfectly good recipe for a sweet treat made of the best ingredients you have, leaving out preservatives or other highly processed substances.

balls of dough on baking sheets. Bake for ten to twelve minutes. The dough puffs a little then settles flat when they are done. Cool.

FROSTING:

- ¾ CUP (1½ STICKS) BUTTER
- 3 CUPS OF CONFECTIONERS' SUGAR
- 3 TABLESPOONS CREAM OR HALF-N-HALF
- 2 TEASPOONS VANILLA EXTRACT

Cream the butter in the mixer, gradually adding the confect-ioner's sugar. Beat for at least a minute, then add cream and vanilla. Beat until fluffy. Spread frosting on one of a pair of cook-ies, then add the other cookie and squeeze lightly to push filling to edge. Yields a variable number of filled cookies depending on size of the cookies. Can be stored, wrapped individually, in freezer.

. . .

Shortbread Plain and Chocolate

You might remember when you were a kid examining a plate of cookies, looking for the ones with the most icing or candy sprinkles. We loved big sugar cookies with lurid icing. Now that I'm a grown-up, shortbreads are the perfect cookie. A plateful delights with a glass of tawney port or sherry.

SHORTBREAD

½ CUP BUTTER, AT ROOM TEMPERATURE

½ CUP CONFECTIONERS' SUGAR, SIFTED TO REMOVE LUMPS

½ TEASPOON VANILLA

1 CUP ALL-PURPOSE FLOUR

2 TABLESPOONS CORNSTARCH

Heat the oven to 325 degrees and line an eight-to-nine-inch square or round pan with parchment paper. Cream the butter and gradually add the confectioners' sugar beating until the mixture is fluffy. Add the vanilla and beat to incorporate it. Sift together the flour and cornstarch and add them gradually to the butter and sugar mixture. When the mixture in the bowl comes together loosely, looking a little like pie dough, distrib-ute it over the bottom of the pan and press it right to the edges making sure that the thickness is even. Prick it all over with a fork and press the fork tines onto the edge all around the pan. Alternatively, press the dough into a half-inch thick square on a baking sheet, prick it all over with a fork, and cut it into smaller squares slightly separated from one another. Bake for thirty to forty minutes, check it to see if it is firm all over but not browned. If it is still a little soft reduce the oven to 300 and give it another five minutes or until it is firm to the touch. Cool

{ADVICE}

« Confectioner's sugar often gets a little lumpy so running it through a sifter is a good idea. Also sifting the flour and cornstarch together mixes them nicely. In the chocolate shortbread, by all means sift the chocolate with the flour and cornstarch.

Generally it isn't necessary to grease pans you bake shortbread in, but I did line my pans with parchment paper.

If you cut the short-bread into fan shapes, know that the triangular tips of each piece are very fragile. Handle them carefully. You can also flatten the dough into a free-standing square on a parchment lined baking sheet to bake it and cut it into squares.

it slightly and while it is still warm, cut it, if it is round, into fan shapes, or any desired shape then let it finish cooling. Lift the individual pieces out of the pan to serve or put away for later.

Chocolate and wine served together is a bit controversial, but some claim Merlot and chocolate together work well. Chocolate shortbreads with a cup of coffee is a perfect pick-me-up.

CHOCOLATE SHORTBREAD

½ CUP BUTTER

½ CUP CONFECTIONERS' SUGAR

¾ CUP ALL-PURPOSE FLOUR

1 TABLESPOON CORNSTARCH

3 TABLESPOONS COCOA POWDER

⅓ CUP CHOCOLATE CHIPS

Follow the assembly instructions above but heat the oven to 300 degrees. Bake for 30 to 40 minutes, test to see if they are firm, and if they are still soft, bake them an additional time until the shortbread can't be dented with a finger.

Hello Dolly Squares and Marjorie Standish

"These are not State-of-Mainish in any way," wrote Marjorie Standish in *Cooking Down East*, 1969, "except just about everyone in Maine makes them." Back in the '60s, when I was busy being an awkward teenager, the whole darn country was apparently making these. And humming along with Carol Channing in the Broadway musical. Is that why they are called Hello Dolly Squares? Maybe. They are also called Magic Squares and there is a version with seven ingredients called Seven Layer Squares.

I bumped into these bars while working on a compilation of Marjorie Standish recipes entitled *Cooking Maine Style*, which appeared in print in 2018. While Mrs. Standish included lots of truly traditional Maine recipes in her columns and books, this one is a thoroughly Modern Millie recipe.

· · ·
"Hello Dolly" Squares

Icky-sticky, tooth-achingly sweet, and an absolute snap to put together, you can memorize this recipe easily because it is one cup of everything except butter which is one stick. It leaves you with a part of a can of sweetened condensed milk which you can use in your coffee or tea if you like milk and sugar added.

Dial back some of the sweetness by using unsweetened coconut flakes and semi-sweet chocolate chips instead of milk chocolate. Mrs. Standish said to cut them into "very small squares," good advice because a little goes a very long way.

- 1 STICK BUTTER
- 1 CUP GRAHAM CRUMBS
- 1 CUP FLAKED COCONUT
- 1 CUP CHOCOLATE BITS
- 1 CUP CHOPPED NUTS
- 1 CUP SWEETENED CONDENSED MILK

Heat an oven to 350 degrees. Melt butter in a nine-by-nine-inch pan. Sprinkle in the graham crackers and mix them around a bit until the butter has soaked into the crumbs. Then sprinkle on coconut, unmelted chocolate bits, and nuts, making sure you have ingredients in each corner. Pour condensed milk on top. Bake for thirty minutes. Cool in pan and cut into very small squares.

⟫⟫⟩ PIES AND GALETES ⟨⟨⟨⟨

· · ·
Galettes and Galette Dough

Just about any pastry for pie works for galettes which are mainly a disk of dough rolled out, topped with fruit filling, and with the rim pulled up to partly cover the still visible filling.

The galette dough which follows, however, is a finer dough, and ramps up the flavor and texture. You can fill it with any combination of fruit you please.

GALETTE DOUGH

1 CUP FLOUR

¼ CUP CORNMEAL

1 TEASPOON SUGAR

½ TEASPOON SALT

7 TABLESPOONS COLD BUTTER, CUT INTO PIECES

3 TABLESPOONS SOUR CREAM

⅓ CUP ICE WATER

Toss together the flour, cornmeal, sugar, and salt, then using a food processor, pastry cutter, or two knives, cut in the butter until you can't see butter bits. Stir together the sour cream and ice water, and add to the flour and butter mixture, tossing until a ball of dough forms. Divide it in two, form a flat disk and chill for an hour or so. Heat the oven to 400 degrees. and lightly grease a baking sheet. Prepare the filling of your choice. Roll out the disks and place on the baking sheet. Pile about two cups of filling in the center of each disk, and fold the edges up and partly over the filling. Bake for forty to fifty minutes, until the filling is soft, and the dough is golden brown. Cool. {Serves 6 to 8}

• • •

Rustic Apple Tart

This dessert looks a lot like a galette. All you need is one pie crust, four or five medium apples, and a jar of jelly or jam. The jelly or jam adds a bit of moisture and flavor to the apples; spread a generous layer on the pastry itself and stir some into the sliced apples. Almost any kind of preserve goes with apples. Use what you have and like.

This little tart can be baked in a pie plate or on a baking sheet.

4 TO 5 MEDIUM APPLES, PEELED, CORED, SPLICED

1 TO 2 TABLESPOONS FLOUR

2 TABLESPOONS WHITE OR LIGHT BROWN SUGAR

¼ TABLESPOON CINNAMON, OR MORE TO TASTE

JELLY OR JAM TO TASTE

{ADVICE}

❮ Our friend George Crouse makes wonderful galettes using chopped dates to sweeten fillings. Rather than add sugar, he chops up three or four dried, pitted dates and adds them to apples or any firm stone fruit that needs a little sweetening.

Heat the oven to 350. Line a nine-inch pie plate with the pastry, or lay it on a parchment covered baking sheet. Put the prepared apples into a medium bowl along with the flour, sugar, and cinnamon, and toss it all together until the apples are lightly coated with flour and sugar. Spread a layer of jelly or jam on the pastry and add an optional dollop to the apple mix and toss the apples to mix in the preserve. Pile the apples in the center of the pastry and gently pull the edges of the pastry up and around the edges of apple, pressing it into place over the apples. There will be an open space at the top. Bake for thirty to forty minutes, or until the apples are tender and the crust is golden brown. *{Makes 1 eight-to-nine-inch tart}*

• • •

cMAPLE SYRUP PIE

Those of us accustomed to finding any ingredient we may want in the store at any time of year might have a hard time envisioning the head scratching among early American housewives trying to figure out what to put in a crust for dessert, during the late spring pie-filling void between the last apples from the previous fall and the first red stalks of rhubarb. Here is a fine example of sugar-based pies.

The recipe that follows is from Jacqueline Huggins in Alton.

1 BAKED 9-INCH PIE SHELL

2 WHOLE EGGS

2 EGG YOLKS

1 CUP BROWN SUGAR

1 CUP WHIPPING CREAM

½ CUP FANCY GRADE MAPLE SYRUP

½ TEASPOON VANILLA EXTRACT

Preheat the oven to 350 degrees. In a medium bowl, lightly beat the eggs and egg yolks. Whisk in the brown sugar, cream, maple syrup, and vanilla. Beat until the sugar is dissolved. Pour into the pie shell. Bake for forty-five to fifty minutes or until the center is nearly firm. Allow it to cool before serving. Top with whipped cream.

. . .

Apple Cranberry Crumble Pie

The crumble topping in this recipe takes the place of a pastry lid and contributes to overall sweetness to off-set the cranberries' sourness. If you have a sweet tooth, you might want to add more brown sugar to the filling, up to three-quarters of a cup.

A variation you may wish to try calls for half fresh cranberries and half dried ones. If you lack fresh cranberries, dried would be a worthy substitute. Add a splash of hot water to the berries before you put them in the pie; the water will plump them slightly.

PASTRY SUFFICIENT TO LINE A NINE-INCH PAN

FILLING:

4 CUPS PEELED, SLICED APPLES, ABOUT 2 POUNDS

2 CUPS CRANBERRIES, ABOUT 8 OUNCES

½ CUP BROWN SUGAR

3 TABLESPOONS FLOUR

¼ TEASPOON GROUND NUTMEG

¼ TEASPOON CINNAMON

CRUMB TOPPING

½ CUP FLOUR

½ CUP ROLLED OATS

⅓ CUP BROWN SUGAR

¼ CUP, OR HALF A STICK, BUTTER, MELTED

Heat the oven to 400 degrees. Line a nine-inch pie plate with the pastry and crimp the edges Toss together all the filling ingredients—apples, cranberries, sugar, flour, and spices and put them in the pie shell.

For the crumb topping, mix flour, oats, and brown sugar into a bowl and mix together. Add the melted butter and stir to blend. Sprinkle the crumb mixture over the top of the filling, spreading to cover evenly. Bake for fifteen minutes at

400 degrees, then reduce the oven to 375 degrees and bake an additional thirty to forty minutes until the pastry and crumb topping are golden and you can see bubbling around the edges. Cool and serve with ice cream or whipped cream.

⋙ FRUITY DESSERTS ⋘

No fooling! Fools are such an easy dessert. A fruit puree, usually berry, folded into whipped cream and allowed to cool, sweetened to taste, and possibly seasoned with lemon juice or an optional light dash of spice, like cinnamon or ginger, makes a remarkably light mid–summer dessert.

. . .

Strawberry Fool

For a specific fool recipe, here is one using strawberries. If you have never made a fool before, follow this one, then extrapolate with the Berry Fool that follows with any other berry you have.

1 PINT OF STRAWBERRIES

A SPRINKLE OF SUGAR

A GRATING OF NUTMEG (OPTIONAL)

CINNAMON (OPTIONAL)

1 CUP OF WHIPPING OR HEAVY CREAM (OR THICK YOGURT,
     SOUR CREAM)

¼ CUP OF SUGAR (MORE OR LESS TO TASTE)

½ TEASPOON VANILLA EXTRACT

Pinch off the green hulls and slice the berries into a bowl. Sprinkle with sugar and optional spices and let stand a few minutes or longer until the juices run. When you are ready to assemble the dish, whip the cream with sugar, adding vanilla when the cream begins to thicken. Spoon about half the strawberries into a food processor and puree them (or mash well with a masher or the back of the spoon against the side of the bowl.) Add the result back to the remaining berries and mix well. Fold that mixture into the whipped cream, blending very well. Serve immediately or put into the fridge until you are ready to serve. *{Makes 3 servings}*

. . .

Berry Fool

1 CUP OF BERRIES, FRESH OR FROZEN

1 TABLESPOON LEMON JUICE, OR LESS TO TASTE

SUGAR TO TASTE

SPICE TO TASTE, OPTIONAL

1 CUP OF WHIPPING CREAM

Simmer the berries briefly just until the juice begins to run, or soften them in the microwave. Strain them through a sieve or food mill to remove most of the seeds. Add the lemon juice, sugar, and optional spice and mix well. Beat the whipping cream until it forms peaks, and then gently fold the berry puree into the cream. Put in serving glasses, and chill for a couple of hours before serving. *{Makes 3 to 4 servings}*

. . .

Blueberry Clafouti

Amazing what happens when you mix milk, eggs, butter, sugar, and flour in varying proportions. From cake to puddings, all you have to do is add more or less of one or another and a whole new dish emerges.

Apparently, the classic clafouti, a French dish, is made with cherries. In Maine's blueberry season, that is the one to use. Cherries or berries are better in this dessert than peaches or apples because it is baked at a low temperature and the berries hold together without bursting.

1 CUP MILK

3 EGGS (PLUS 1 YOLK, OPTIONAL)

⅓ TO ½ CUP SUGAR

1 TEASPOON VANILLA EXTRACT

3 TABLESPOONS BUTTER, MELTED

½ CUP FLOUR
1 CUP BLUEBERRIES

Heat the oven to 325 degrees. Put the milk, eggs, sugar, vanilla, and melted butter together in a bowl and whisk it all together until it is smooth. Continue to whisk and add the flour gradually. The batter should be smooth. Add the blueberries and stir batter to distribute them evenly. Pour into a greased baking dish or skillet and bake for thirty to thirty-five minutes. It will puff up and a knife inserted comes out clean. Serve warm, dusted with confectioners' sugar. {Makes 4 to 6 servings}

. . .

Very Crisp Peach Cobbler

If a peach crisp and a peach cobbler got married this recipe would be their off-spring.

Yes, you can grow peaches in Maine, and even if it isn't Georgia, any ripe peach just off the tree is going to taste vastly better than any peach that has traveled from distant parts to cool its heels in the produce department of some grocery store.

Meg DeKoslowski, who visited here from Maryland, gave me her grandmother's recipe for this cobbler, which combines a semi-batter topping with a crisp's sweet crunch. She recommended making it in a nine-by-thirteen pan, which creates a thin layer of peach with the topping, but you could put it in a smaller one to end up with a slightly thicker layer of peaches and denser top. Mixing beaten egg into a sugar and flour mix creates a loose, crumble-like result. The crumble rises with the baking powder in it, covers the peaches, and the sugar and melted butter poured over the top bake together for a crunchy, sweet, almost cookie-like crust.

MEG'S GRANNY'S PEACH COBBLER
4 TO 6 CUPS OF SLICED, RIPE PEACHES
JUICE OF HALF A LEMON
½ CUP WHITE SUGAR
½ CUP LIGHT BROWN SUGAR
1 CUP FLOUR

2 TEASPOONS BAKING POWDER

½ TEASPOON CINNAMON OR MORE TO TASTE

1 EGG

1 TEASPOON VANILLA EXTRACT

½ CUP OR ONE STICK BUTTER, MELTED

VANILLA ICE CREAM OR WHIPPED CREAM, OPTIONAL

Heat the oven to 375 degrees and lightly grease a nine-thirteen-inch baking dish. Distribute the peaches over the bottom of the dish, and sprinkle lemon juice over them. Whisk together sugars, flour, baking powder, and cinnamon. Beat the egg with a fork and add the vanilla and mix into the dry ingredients. Mix until all the flour is taken up, rubbing it together with your fingers or the back of a spoon. Distribute the flour mixture evenly over the top of the peaches. Spoon the melted butter over all. Bake for thirty to thirty-five minutes, until the top is golden brown and the peaches are bubbling. Serve warm with or without ice cream or whipped cream. *{Makes 6 to 8 servings}*

• • •

Knobby Apple Cake

This recipe came from the late Karyl Bannister on West Southport Island where for a long time, she published a dandy newsletter called "Cook 'n Tell." She had a great knack for finding easy recipes for tasty and practical home-cooking.

This cake will take any apple you throw at it, cut into chunks roughly no larger than a half-inch. You don't have to peel the apples unless you want to, and while the recipe calls for three cups of apples, you can figure on using three to four medium-sized apples, and round it up or down to the nearest whole apple.

It calls for nutmeg; you can certainly use cinnamon. Sprinkle cinnamon sugar on the top. The dough is tough and bumpy but it tolerates being pushed around. Just cram it into a pan and jam it into the corners and you will be all set. Ultimately, the cake tastes like you did much more than the recipe seems to call for. Serve with whipped cream.

1 CUP FLOUR

1 TEASPOON BAKING SODA

½ TEASPOON GRATED NUTMEG

PINCH OF SALT

1 CUP SUGAR

2 TABLESPOONS BUTTER

1 EGG

1 TEASPOON VANILLA

3 CUPS DICED APPLES

CINNAMON SUGAR, OPTIONAL

Heat the oven to 350 degrees. Grease an eight-by-eight inch pan. Whisk or sift together the flour, baking soda, nutmeg and salt. Set aside. Cream together the sugar and butter and beat in the egg. Add the chopped apples and vanilla and mix well so all the apples have some of the sugar, butter, and egg mixture on them. Add the flour mixture and toss together until the flour is taken up. Put into the baking pan, spread evenly. Sprinkle the top of the batter with cinnamon sugar to taste. Bake for thirty-five to forty minutes or until a tester inserted comes out clean. Let cool slightly, then serve warm. *{Makes 1 8-inch cake}*

. . .

PINEAPPLE UPSIDE DOWN CAKE

Keep a can of crushed pineapple or rings on hand and the ingredients for a simple cake, and this gooey delicious dessert can be yours for a few minutes of stirring, arranging, and baking time.

I picked this recipe up sometime in 1970, one of the first recipes I ever collected and very popular with the youngsters in a family I lived with when I first left home. My Millennial aged niece Sarah acquires a rapturous look when I make it, just as she did when she was a teen. It's a keeper.

If you have a cast-iron skillet, use it; it moves easily from stove-top butter-melting to oven-baking. Sometimes recipes call for maraschino cherries in the center of each pineapple ring; you can substitute dried or fresh cranberries.

Pineapple Cake's Evolution

The Dole Company raised and canned so much pineapple in the first decades of the 1900s that, to help create demand, the Dole test kitchen worked up recipes that home cooks could use. An apple upside-down-cake in general use at the time probably evolved into Pineapple Upside Down Cake which has been in use for a hundred years.

¼ CUP BUTTER

1 CUP BROWN SUGAR

1 CAN OF PINEAPPLE RINGS

FRESH OR DRIED CRANBERRIES, OPTIONAL.

3 TABLESPOONS BUTTER

1 CUP GRANULATED SUGAR

2 EGGS

1½ CUPS FLOUR

1½ TEASPOON BAKING POWDER

½ CUP MILK

Heat the oven to 350 degrees. In a heavy pan, a ten-inch skillet or baking pan, melt the quarter cup of butter and add the brown sugar , stirring them together and spreading to cover the bottom of the pan. Lay the pineapple slices on top of the melted butter and sugar. Put cherries or cranberries in the center of the rings. Cream together the three tablespoons of butter and sugar, then beat in the eggs. Whisk the flour and baking powder and add to the butter, eggs, and sugar mixture alternately with the milk to make a smooth batter. Pour the batter over the top of the pineapples and bake for forty to fifty minutes until it is golden and the center feels firm to the touch. Allow it to cool slightly, run a knife around the perimeter of the cake, then place a plate on the top of the pan, and invert it quickly. If necessary, scrape up a little of the butter and sugar and spread it back on the pineapple. {Makes a 10-inch cake}

FROZEN DESSERTS

It's freezing...desserts, that is. Sorbet, gelato, and sherbet are easily made in a home kitchen, with or without an ice cream freezer.

Sorbet is more intensely flavored than gelato and gelato is a bit smoother and aromatic. The recipe that follows calls for strawberries, though the recipe can employ most berries.

• • •

Strawberry Sorbet

½ CUP WATER
½ CUP SUGAR
2 CUPS STRAWBERRY PUREE
JUICE OF 1 LEMON

Mix these together and chill very well. Put into the ice cream maker and freeze until very thick or freeze in a stainless steel bowl and scrape down the sides periodically until you have your desired consistency. Pack into a container and keep frozen until use. *{Makes a scant quart}*

• • •

Strawberry Gelato

Out in Monroe, Sharon Smith wrote, "Have a recipe to share for strawberry gelato." She reported that she found the gelato recipe in a favorite cookbook by Marcella Hazan but she made a variation using low fat yogurt, and said, "It was just as good as the version with cream. Couldn't tell the difference."

It's great to have something cool and flavorful that doesn't pack on the fat.

½ POUND FRESH STRAWBERRIES
¾ CUP SUGAR
¾ CUP WATER
¼ CUP COLD WHIPPING CREAM OR LOW-FAT YOGURT

Prepare the strawberries by hulling and halving them, if large. Put berries and sugar into a food processor, process for a few moments; then add the water and continue to process until they are liquefied. Put into a mixing bowl. Whip the cream until it thickens slightly then fold it or the yogurt into the strawberry mixture. Chill very well before using the ice cream maker. Keep frozen until use. *{Yields a pint and a half, about four servings}*

. . .

Tangy Lemon Sherbet

Here is a stunningly simple recipe for dessert. You don't even have to have an ice cream maker, although one helps the process. The recipe comes from friend and island neighbor Kathy Kerr and is exactly the right thing after a rich meal.

You can use an ice cream maker if you have one. Alternatively, all you have to do is put the sherbet mixture into the freezer, contained in a bowl like a wide, stainless-steel bowl, with fairly thin sides or baking pan. Visit the sherbet every half hour or so to stir it up until it is frozen but smooth.

If you prefer a slightly sourer sherbet, add lemon zest and a few drops of lemon extract. The yellow food coloring could be optional. Left to its own devices, the sherbet is more or less white, and if you don't care whether it is lemony-looking or not, you can leave the coloring out.

Incidentally, you can use lactose-free or plant-based milk to make this sherbet.

> 2 CUPS OF MILK
> 2 CUPS OF WATER
> 2 CUPS OF SUGAR
> ½ CUP LEMON JUICE
> 2 DROPS OF YELLOW FOOD COLORING (OPTIONAL)
> ZEST OF ONE OR TWO LEMONS (OPTIONAL)
> 1 TEASPOON LEMON EXTRACT (OPTIONAL)

Put all the ingredients into a bowl and mix until the sugar is completely dissolved. Freeze in an ice cream maker, or pour into a metal or glass bowl, or large metal baking pan, and put into the freezer. Periodically, scrape congealed sherbet from the sides of the bowl or pan toward the center. Continue this process until all the mixture is frozen and stir a few times more to break up any icy chunks that form. *{Makes about a quart and a half of sherbet}*

CHOCOLATE ICE CREAM

My actual all-time favorite homemade ice cream is an old recipe from a cookbook printed in 1882, Mary Henderson's Chocolate Ice Cream from *Practical Cooking and Dinner Giving*.

With this recipe, you must do the whole custard-making thing; chill it, whip cream, fold it in, and then churn it. A lot of people have electric churns these days with the drum that you stick in the freezer ahead of time to provide the chilling. So even if you don't exert yourself to the extent of cranking, you still have to put effort into making this ice cream. It's worth it. The result is a creamy premium ice cream with a rich, chocolaty flavor.

2 CUPS MILK

1 CUP SUGAR

4 OUNCES UNSWEETENED BAKING CHOCOLATE

6 EGG YOLKS

1 TEASPOON GELATIN DISSOLVED IN 2 TABLESPOONS WATER

2 TEASPOONS VANILLA

2 CUPS WHIPPING OR HEAVY CREAM

In a double boiler or a very heavy saucepan, scald the milk. When bubbles appear around the edges of the pan, add the sugar, and stir until it is dissolved. Add the chocolate broken up—and melt it in the milk and sugar, stirring the mixture from time to time, until it is all dissolved. In a separate bowl, beat the egg yolks, and then add a half cup or so of the hot milk and sugar to the eggs; stir them together and then add the tempered eggs to the rest of milk in the pan. Watching carefully, and keeping the temperature at a medium heat, stir the egg and milk mixture until it thickens, and coats the back of a spoon. Add the gelatin and vanilla and chill the custard until it is very cold. When you are ready to freeze the ice cream, whip the cream until it makes soft peaks, fold it into the custard, and freeze it in your ice cream maker according to the churn directions. *{Makes about a quart of ice cream}*

. . .

BANANA CREAM FREEZE

This frozen dessert came from an old James Beard cookbook, the first cookbook I acquired about fifty years ago. I wish I could tell you the name, but the cover and title page is long-gone along with most of the index. This recipe has proven to be very handy.

Because super-ripe bananas are so sweet, lemon or lime juice is absolutely necessary. You can add spices like cinnamon, cloves, or nutmeg, dribble in some rum, or add some coconut, toasted or not. Using raw or light brown sugar in this recipe deepens the flavor.

The initial steps are very easy. Stirring the mixture occasionally while it freezes, while not an onerous task, means you must plan ahead to allow time for the mixture to firm up.

2 TO 3 OVER-RIPE BANANAS
½ CUP SUGAR
JUICE OF 1 LEMON OR LIME, ABOUT 2 TABLESPOONS
SPICE TO TASTE, OPTIONAL
RUM OR FLAVOR EXTRACT TO TASTE, OPTIONAL
¼ CUP COCONUT, OPTIONAL
½ PINT WHIPPING CREAM

Mash the bananas well, add the sugar, lemon or lime juice, and optional ingredients. In a separate bowl, beat the whipping cream until soft peaks form, and fold into the banana mixture. Put the mixture into a container that you can freeze (a glass or stainless-steel bowl works well). Put in the freezer. Give it a stir every hour or so at least twice then allow it to freeze through. *{Serves 4}*

6
CELEBRATE!

Some holidays appear on the calendar. Others appear in lavish displays at the end of grocery store aisles in a run-up to the day itself. Lots of holidays have significant food associations: Easter eggs, Thanksgiving turkey, Christmas cookies.

For example, Super Bowl is declared by the National Football League, the date is set for early February, and grocery stores pile beer, chips, and three-alarm chili kits at the ends of the aisles. Friends gather to watch the game, eat, and drink. It's a holiday all right, even if it's not printed on the calendar.

Valentine's Day qualifies as a holiday if you observe it from a commercial point of view, with flowers, jewelry, especially diamond rings, and cards being snapped up. It ought to be National Chocolate Day, but in fact October 28th is! (The 28th ought to be National Candy Corn Day, don't you think?)

St. Patrick's Day brings corned beef and heads of cabbage into stores. You don't have to be Irish to drink Guiness and enjoy soda bread.

Lots of people gather at Easter even if religious observance isn't part of the day. Stores stock up on hams and egg dyeing kits, and some families recall their ethnic heritage with special baked goods.

In Maine, because it isn't a federal holiday, Patriots Day rolls around in April, con-fusingly closing town offices and banks while stores and the post office carry on. There is no discernible holiday food associated with the commemoration of the Battles at Concord and Lexington that started the American Revolutionary War. We'll find patriotism, though, in Fourth of July menus in conjunction with the start of summer's casual fare for picnic and backyard gatherings.

In the last six weeks of the calendar year, we really pile on the holidays and their foods, starting with Thanksgiving and winding up on New Year's. We bake and make and entertain, and fall into happy, overfed heaps, making reso-lutions to spend January eating salad and going to the gym.

How wonderful it all is.

SUPER BOWL FOOD

Finger food is best for Super Bowl treats. Pass the napkins with the dips and the satay-style wings that follow.

. . .

Pat's Corn Dip

Pat Mitchell, Islesboro neighbor, brought this dip to a holiday party, and I had a hard time keeping my snout, er, nose, out of it. She kindly sent me the recipe a couple of days later.

It's quick to assemble, especially if you keep a little four-ounce can of green chilies on hand. Keeping a can of white corn that the recipe calls for means you can put it together without a trip to the store. As far as the chili and red pepper flakes are concerned, it's a matter of personal taste. Use them or not. If you are hanging with a twelve-alarm chili crowd, well, dump it in. If you belong to the milk toast end of the spectrum, leave it out.

8 OUNCES OF CREAM CHEESE

2½ CUPS GRATED CHEESE, CHEDDAR, MONTEREY JACK, OR PARMESAN

½ CUP SOUR CREAM

2 CUPS WHITE CORN KERNELS

½ CUP, OR 4 OUNCES, DICED GREEN CHILIES

½ TEASPOON CHILI POWDER

1 TO 2 CLOVES MINCED GARLIC

½ TEASPOON SALT

RED PEPPER FLAKES TO TASTE

1 MEDIUM TOMATO

4 TO 5 SCALLIONS

BUNDLE OF CILANTRO

Heat the oven to 350 degrees and grease a medium casserole or a nine-by-thirteen glass baking pan. Mix together all the cheese, sour cream, corn and chilies and blend thoroughly. Stir in chili powder, garlic, salt, and red pepper flakes and pour into the casserole or baking pan. Bake for thirty minutes.

Meanwhile, dice the tomatoes, chop the scallions and cilantro, and toss together in a bowl. Set aside. Remove the dip from the oven and let cool slightly before adding the vegetable topping. Serve with sturdy corn chips, or crudités.

. . .

Rotel Dip

A summertime neighbor, Muffet Moran, showed me how to put together Rotel Dip, named after Rotel vegetables, the canned tomato and chili mixture easy to find at the grocery store. Annoyingly delicious and too easy to make, the recipe below has three ingredients and only one of them requires effort on the cook's part. You'll need a can opener, a pair of scissors, and fingers supple enough to open a package of cream cheese and one of bulk sausage.

Assembly cooking, where one takes several essentially pre-pared foods and combines them to make a new dish, is just the ticket when you are preparing for a big party, either during the holidays or on Game Day.

It isn't supposed to be wholesome or even good-looking. It's supposed to taste good and be scoopable with a tortilla chip.

If you follow the assembly directions below, you will make about three cups, which is to say, not enough.

1 POUND OF GROUND BEEF OR PREPARED BULK SAUSAGE

1 10-OUNCE CAN OF ROTEL VEGETABLES

½ POUND OR 1 8-OUNCE PACKAGE OF CREAM CHEESE

TORTILLA CHIPS OR SCOOPS

BROWN THE MEAT IN A HEAVY SAUCEPAN.

ADD THE VEGETABLES AND STIR THEM IN, LETTING THEM SIMMER A LITTLE
    WHILE, ABOUT FIVE MINUTES.

Add the cream cheese and let it melt. Stir all together and allow to thicken. Serve warm with corn chips. {*Yields 3½ cups*}

Satay-Style Chicken Wings

This way of preparing wings is a grand alternative to Buffalo Wings.

Coconut milk, light cream, half-and-half or evaporated milk thins the peanut butter and keeps the sauce thick. Try to use the smooth kind of peanut butter made from only peanuts and salt—no sugar or other fats added.

You'll bake the wings twice, once to cook them, and once to bake on the peanut sauce. If you like it, consider adding chipotle powder to the sauce. Alternatively, consider doubling the peanut sauce recipe that follows. Set aside half to bake the wings with, then add chipotle, chili powder, or hot Thai sauce to the other half to serve as dipping sauce. That way capsicum cowards like me can enjoy the wings without any pain.

> 3 TO 5 POUNDS OF CHICKEN WINGS
>
> ⅓ CUP COCONUT MILK OR HALF-AND-HALF
>
> ⅓ CUP SMOOTH PEANUT BUTTER
>
> 2 TABLESPOONS SOY OR TAMARI SAUCE
>
> JUICE OF HALF A LIME
>
> CHIPOTLE POWDER, CHILI POWDER, OR RED PEPPER FLAKES TO TASTE
>   (OPTIONAL)

Disjoint the chicken wings into three pieces, reserve the two larger parts; save the tips to make stock if you wish. Heat the oven to 375 degrees. Put the wing pieces on a rack in a roasting pan and bake for fifteen minutes, turn them over and bake another fifteen minutes. Whisk together the milk, peanut butter, soy sauce, and lime juice, plus optional spice powder. Put the already-baked wing pieces in a large bowl and pour the peanut sauce over them and toss until the wings are well-coated. Return to the oven and bake an additional fifteen minutes per side. Reserve any leftover sauce for dipping. Serve warm or at room temperature. {*Makes a scant cup of sauce, enough for 3 to 5 pounds of wings*}

VALENTINE CHOCOLATE

. . .

Chocolate Bark

Chocolate bark calls merely for melted chocolate, into which you stir chopped nuts, candied fruit, or crushed candy. Match the chocolate to your chocolate preference: milk, semi-sweet, or dark. A solid cooking chocolate bar found online, or a better quality chocolate found in most grocery store baking sections is the way to go. You can use pistachios and sunflower and pumpkin seeds that you roast in a heavy skillet over a medium heat just until they turn a golden tinge. If almonds or pecans appeal to you, substitute them for the pistachios. You could even sprinkle on dried cranberries.

CHOCOLATE BARK WITH NUTS AND SEEDS
8 OUNCES CHOCOLATE, BROKEN OR CHOPPED FAIRLY SMALL
½ CUP PISTACHIOS, OR ALMONDS, WALNUTS, OR PECANS CHOPPED
½ CUP DRY-ROASTED PUMPKIN SEEDS AND SUNFLOWER SEEDS

Use parchment paper to line a baking pan or sheet. Heat water in a pan and put the chocolate in a bowl set in the hot water. Keep the water hot but don't let it boil. Gradually melt the chocolate, stirring until it all melts and is smooth. Stir the nuts and seeds into the melted chocolate, making sure they are thoroughly coated. Spread evenly on the parchment covered pan and set away to chill. Cut or break into serving-sized pieces.

. . .

Chocolate Pie

This recipe came from Sue Stafford, an Islesboro neighbor, who brought it to a holiday potluck. The pie remains firm when cut, sagging very little where other chocolate pies tend to be pudding-like. All the butter firms up and keeps the confectioner's sugar and egg in line, and the melted chocolate stiffens to add structure.

➤ *For the chocolate pie filling, it is a really good idea to have the butter fairly soft, but not melted, when you cream it together with the confectioner's sugar so that it smooths out nicely. Using your mixer is a good plan, and as you add the chocolate and beaten eggs, make sure you beat it all very well to keep it creamy. The melted chocolate has to be cool but still liquid; check it from time to time to make sure it stays soft, and beat well as you add it. If you need to soften the chocolate, put it back over the hot water for a few moments.*

Sue was pleased to discover a great way to stabilize the whipped cream, and the directions for doing that are included below.

Using chocolate graham crackers for the crumb crust is just the ticket and works better than a chocolate cookie crust. The graham crackers have quite a bit of sugar in them, so less confectioner's is better unless you have a great sweet tooth.

CHOCOLATE GRAHAM CRACKER CRUST:

1½ CUP CHOCOLATE GRAHAM CRACKERS, CRUSHED INTO FINE CRUMBS

¼ TO ⅓ CUP OF CONFECTIONER'S SUGAR

6 OUNCES OF BUTTER MELTED

Heat an oven to 350 degrees. Put the cracker crumbs and sugar into a bowl and mix well. Add the melted butter very gradually, stirring to combine. Press crumbs and butter mixture over the bottom of a pie plate and up the sides. Bake for 10 minutes. {Sufficient for a 9-inch pie}

CHOCOLATE FILLING:

4 OUNCES UNSWEETENED BAKING CHOCOLATE

1 CUP OR 2 STICKS BUTTER

2 CUPS CONFECTIONERS' SUGAR

½ TEASPOON VANILLA

4 EGGS

Melt the chocolate and let cool. Cream the butter and sugar; beat vigorously. Add the chocolate and vanilla. Beat well. Add the eggs and beat. Pour into the pie shell and chill two to three hours.

WHIPPED CREAM TOPPING:

1 CUP HEAVY CREAM

1 TABLESPOON CORN STARCH

SUGAR TO TASTE

Whisk together the cup of heavy cream and the tablespoon of corn starch in a heavy bottom saucepan. Bring the mixture slowly to a boil, stirring constantly. Once it comes to a boil, boil thirty seconds longer. Chill; it will be thick. Whip until it is thick enough to spread, adding some sugar to sweeten it as you would for regular whipped cream. Spread over the top of the pie. *{Makes about 1¹/₂ to 2 cups whipped cream}*

⇛ ST. PATRICK'S DAY ⬺

. . .

IRISH POUND CAKE

The proudly Irish Islesboro matriarch, Eileen Shea Boardman, gave me this recipe. When Eileen passed away, I took this cake to the reception following her memorial service. We miss Eileen and remember her with this cake.

Now, I hate to say that probably the reason it is called Irish is less because it hails from the Old Sod, than it contains Irish Mist or Irish whiskey in which we soak the golden raisins. Once baked, just the slight hint of whiskey flavor is left behind while the alcohol all evaporates.

When this comes out of the oven, it has a lovely crusty exterior. It is perfect to eat with a cup of tea or coffee. Probably even good with a shot of whiskey.

GRATED PEEL OF 1 LEMON

1 CUP GOLDEN RAISINS

3 TABLESPOONS IRISH MIST OR WHISKEY

1 CUP BUTTER

1 CUP SUGAR

4 EGGS

1 TEASPOON VANILLA

2 CUPS FLOUR

½ TEASPOON SALT

¾ TEASPOON BAKING POWDER

Heat the oven to 325. Grease a nine-by-five-inch loaf pan, flour it, and line the bottom with a piece of lightly-greased parchment paper. Put the lemon zest and raisins in a small bowl and dribble the whiskey over it, tossing to coat. Cream together the butter and sugar until the mixture is fluffy. Add the eggs, beating well after each addition. Lift the raisins and zest with a slotted spoon and put into a separate bowl and add the whiskey and vanilla to the egg mixture. Whisk the flour, salt, and baking powder together and mix the flour into the egg, sugar, and butter mixture, stirring only enough to blend. Toss the raisins with a little flour and fold into the batter. Bake for an hour and ten minutes, test for doneness, and bake until golden, slightly cracked along the top, and until a tester inserted comes out clean.

• • •
IRISH SODA BREAD AND SOME VARIATIONS

It's too bad that we make Irish Soda Bread for St. Paddy's day and tend to forget it the rest of the year. Similar to making biscuits, you can whip soda bread together in very little time and have it hot at the table, spread with butter melting into it.

What you'll find below is a basic butter and egg enriched soda bread, adapted from a very old *Joy of Cooking*. If you want sweeter bread, add the optional sugar, perhaps even more of it, up to two tablespoons, and choose raisins or currants, or caraway.

When to eat soda bread? First off, as soon the bread comes hot out of the oven. At breakfast with butter and marmalade. Late morning with coffee. At lunch with some cheddar cheese and soup. At tea time in the afternoon with more butter and jam or jelly. At supper with Irish stew or shepherd's pie. Mainly, eat it all of it the day you bake it because, like biscuits, it isn't stellar the second day.

2 CUPS ALL-PURPOSE FLOUR

½ TEASPOON SALT

1½ TEASPOONS BAKING POWDER

½ TEASPOON BAKING SODA

1 TABLESPOON LIGHT BROWN SUGAR, OPTIONAL

¼ CUP OR ½ STICK OF COLD BUTTER

½ CUP CURRANTS OR RAISINS, OPTIONAL

1 TEASPOON CARAWAY SEEDS, OPTIONAL

1 EGG, LIGHTLY BEATEN

⅔ CUP BUTTERMILK

Heat the oven to 325 degrees and grease an eight-inch round pan. Whisk together the flour, salt, baking powder, and optional sugar in a large bowl. Cut or rub in the butter until it looks like coarse cornmeal, or process the butter and dry ingredients together briefly in a food processor. Toss in the optional currants or raisins and/or caraway. Make a well in the flour and butter mixture and add the egg and buttermilk. Stir them together quickly so the dry ingredients are incorporated. Knead the dough lightly in the bowl and turn into the greased pan, pressing the dough to the edges. Slash a cross in the top to allow expansion, brush the top with milk or cream and bake for thirty-five to forty minutes, until it is golden and a tester inserted comes out clean. Serve hot. {Yields 1 8-inch loaf}

Fitzgibbon's A Taste of Ireland

Theodora Fitzgibbon authored one of my favorite books on Irish food traditions, A Taste of Ireland. It's one of a series of "Tastes of" various parts of the British Isles, with recipes she collected.

She reported the coddle, a gentle little stew of ham or bacon and sausages with potato and onion, was a Saturday night favorite; and it dates to the 1700s and probably used oats and leeks before the potatoes and onions replaced them. Beef Braised in Stout also comes from the book.

I like her books because they often include very old, traditional dishes, which have otherwise disappeared, many perfectly good and fun to make. For example, in the Irish book is pratie oaten—mashed potatoes and oatmeal mixed, kneaded well together then rolled or patted out, cut and baked like pancakes on a griddle, and eaten for breakfast with bacon and eggs. They taste better than they sound.

Besides recipes, the books are chock full of historic, many later-nineteenth and early-twentieth century photographs of places and people, street scenes, farms and waterfronts, even the occasional interior shot of a kitchen: iron pots hanging over a peat fire. Even though many of the pictures were taken forty to fifty years after the Great Famine, I can see how life could have been hard indeed, and for an Irish man or woman a trans-Atlantic trip, daunting as it may have been, going to an unknown country might have been preferable to toughing it out in the Irish countryside.

• • •
DUBLIN CODDLE

Even though much traditional Irish cooking leans heavily on spuds, onions or leeks, and oats in various forms—ground, rolled, cut—pork, ham, and sausage also graced Irish tables of the Auld Sod. Food writer Theodora Fitzgibbon says to serve it with soda bread and stout or Guinness.

You can prepare this on the stove or in the oven, covered and simmered slowly, to cook the potatoes through without turning them into mush. The flavor of the coddle depends on the quality of the ham and sausage you use. Traditional Irish (and English) sausages usually contain breadcrumbs which gives them a very different texture from American sausages; you'll want to use whatever is easily available. Thyme, marjoram, and black pepper commonly season sausage, so you can enhance the flavor by adding those to the coddle if your sausages are a little plain. A good, smoky ham is just right, or good quality, smoky thick cut bacon

The onions in this recipe are not just for the flavor but are part of the substance of the dish. The potatoes round it out and turn the coddle into comfort food. If you don't have Guinness or stout, use dark beer.

To coddle the mixture, it helps to cover the ingredients with a piece of parchment paper before you put a lid on the saucepan or casserole for top-stove simmering or baking at a low temperature.

8 SMALL SLICES OF HAM, OR BACON ¼ INCH THICK, CUT INTO PIECES

8 PORK SAUSAGES

4 CUPS OF BOILING WATER

4 LARGE ONIONS SLICED

2 POUNDS OF POTATO, PEELED AND SLICED ONE-HALF-INCH THICK

SALT AND PEPPER

THYME AND MARJORAM, OPTIONAL

Heat the oven to 200 degrees. Put the ham and sausages into a large bowl and pour the boiling hot water over them. Let it soak for about five minutes. Remove the meats and put them into a heavy saucepan or baking dish, reserving the soaking liquid. Put

the sliced onions and potatoes on top of the meat, add salt and
pepper and the thyme and marjoram, if used. Add enough of the
soaking liquid to come half-way up the meat and potatoes. Put a
lid on the saucepan or casserole dish. If you cook it on the stove
top, simmer at a very low temperature, or put it into the oven at
for about an hour or until the potatoes are tender but not mushy

• • •

BEEF BRAISED IN STOUT

Let *them* eat corned beef. Instead, just for a change, let's have
some beef braised in good old Irish stout with onions, carrots,
and prunes simmered alongside. This is pretty heavily adapted
from Theodora Fitzgibbon. Two really important things are,
first, the stout, and second, prunes. You can use a Maine brewed
oatmeal stout. The original recipe called for a half cup of stout
with equal amount of water; I used a half of a bottle because I
kept adding stout as the cooking liquid wasted away. Even so,
the dish requires only part of a bottle, so you or someone in your
household will just have to drink the rest. Prunes, added to the
cooking liquid where they soak up the rich juices, are absolutely
heavenly, so even if it seems odd to use them, don't skip that
ingredient.

    2 TABLESPOONS VEGETABLE OIL
    3 BAY LEAVES
    1½ TO 2 POUNDS OF STEWING OR BRAISING BEEF, CUT INTO
        SERVING-SIZED PIECES
    1 LARGE ONION, SLICED
    2 TABLESPOONS FLOUR, OPTIONAL
    ½ CUP STOUT
    ½ CUP WATER
    1 CUP PITTED PRUNES
    2 TO 3 CARROTS, SLICED CROSSWISE
    SALT AND PEPPER TO TASTE

Heat the vegetable oil in a heavy cook pot with a lid and add the
bay leaves. Heat them for about a minute or two. Add the beef,
and brown on both sides. Add the onions and cook until they

soften, then pull the beef and onions to one side of the pot and sprinkle the optional flour on the fat in the pan. Whisk until smooth then spread the beef and onions back over the bottom of the pan. Add the stout and water and cover. Simmer the beef for about an hour at a low temperature, checking occasionally to make sure there is liquid bubbling in the pan. Add more stout and water if it dries out. Add the prunes, sliced carrots, and more stout and/or water and cover the pan again and continue simmering until the sauce has thickened and the carrots are tender. Taste the sauce and add salt and pepper to taste.

⟫⟫⟫ EASTER ⟪⟪⟪

Europe and Eastern Europe are home to a delectable array of yeast-raised sweet cakes and buns. Here are two to mark the day.

• • •

TSOUREKIA OR POLISH BABKA

Evan Kanarakis, born to Greek and Polish parents, grew up in Australia. He shared his mother's Easter bread recipe, observing that the Greek Easter bread and Polish Babka were very similar. "Somewhat like a brioche," he wrote, "but dependent upon various cooks' specific tastes and preferences as to whether or not it is an especially soft or firmer bread, it will traditionally contain one or more red-dyed hard-boiled eggs still in their shell placed within the dough prior to baking to symbolize, of course, the blood of Christ and rebirth. Here is my mother's recipe."

Evan went on to say that he's seen variations on the tsoureki/babka recipe that call for ingredients like orange juice, rosewater, anise, and cinnamon, and sometimes covered with blanched almonds as well.

3 ENVELOPES YEAST POWDER

1 CUP WARM WATER

1 CUP WARM MILK

1 TEASPOON SUGAR

10 TO 12 CUPS OF PLAIN FLOUR

7 EGGS

1 CUP SUGAR

1 TABLESPOON VANILLA EXTRACT

1 CUP MELTED BUTTER (OR HALF BUTTER/HALF MARGARINE)

In a medium-sized bowl, dissolve yeast in warm water; then add warm milk, one teaspoon sugar, and two cups of flour. Stir, cover, set in warm place for one hour until batter doubles in size and is bubbly. Set the bowl over a saucepan full of hot water and beat together six eggs, sugar, and vanilla. Add melted butter slowly. Stir mixture into yeast batter and add remaining flour using a wooden spoon, reserving one cup for kneading. Mix until mixture comes away from bowl; then tip onto a floured surface and knead until elastic. Place in a large, buttered bowl and brush lightly with melted butter. Cover with a cloth and let it rise in a warm place until double, about two hours. Cut dough into three even-sized portions and shape each portion into a loaf, or alternatively, divide each into three pieces, roll them into a rope and braid them loosely. Place each of the three onto a greased baking pan and cover. Let rise for an hour. Heat the oven to 350 degrees. Brush each bread with beaten egg. Press an egg in and sprinkle sesame seeds or sliced almonds and granulated sugar and bake for twenty-five to thirty minutes.

. . .

Buchteln, Sweet Buns, for Easter Brunch

Ruth Thurston in Machias sent in this recipe for Buchteln, famous in Vienna, saying that her family enjoyed them and she thought others might, too. How could we not like them: tender dough with eggs, butter, and sugar beaten in, a little deposit of jam in the center, served with a bit of butter, a cup of coffee or tea. Perfect.

A mixer's dough hook can handle sticky dough better than hands can. An hour's rising, then punch it down and divide it into eighteen little balls, which you flatten to the size of your palm to hold the jam spooned on them. It takes just a little practice to pull the dough up around the filling and seal it all in. If you miss sealing a couple, the worst that can happen is that those buns stick to the baking pan. While the recipe calls for apricot jam, you could fill with marmalade, peach jam, or whatever you've got.

3½ CUPS FLOUR

1 TABLESPOON YEAST DISSOLVED IN ¼ CUPS WATER

¾ CUP MILK, WARMED

1 EGG PLUS 1 YOLK

1 TEASPOON SALT

RIND OF 1 LEMON, GRATED

1 STICK OF BUTTER

APRICOT JAM, OR YOUR CHOICE

CONFECTIONER'S SUGAR, OPTIONAL

Mix all the ingredients together, except for the jam and confectioner's sugar. Beat well to make sure everything is well incorporated. The dough will be sticky. Let rise covered with a damp cloth until doubled. Turn out on a slightly floured board and divide into eighteen little balls. Flatten each, placing a teaspoon of jam in the center. Pull the dough up around the jam and pinch it shut to seal in the jam. Put seam side down in two greased nine-by-nine pans to let rise again. Heat the oven to 375 degrees. When the buns have doubled, then melt a tablespoon or so of butter and brush the tops of the buns with it. Bake for about thirty minutes; then check to see if they have a golden brown top and/or sound a little hollow when you tap them gently. Sprinkle with confectioner's sugar while still warm. Best eaten while warm.

FOURTH OF JULY

If you garden and got on the stick early enough in April, you might have new peas on the Fourth to go with salmon, one traditional meal for the day. Or you might rather gather with friends for one of the first cookouts of the year with burgers, hot dogs, steaks, or chicken. The Fire Department on Islesboro always has a chicken barbecue with cole slaw and potato salad.

It's a good time for deviled eggs, stacked hot dogs, indoors or out, and for dessert, a cake that looks like Old Glory.

. . .

Deviled Eggs Three Ways

HERBY DEVILED EGGS

BOILED EGGS, SLICED AND YOLKS REMOVED

MAYONNAISE

CRUMBLED DRIED OR FINELY-CHOPPED FRESH DILL LEAVES

FRESH PARSLEY, FINELY CHOPPED

DASH OF GARLIC POWDER

SALT AND PEPPER

Mash the yolks and mix in mayonnaise to a smooth consistency. Mix in the herbs and add salt and pepper to taste. Stuff the egg whites. Garnish with a sprig of dill or parsley.

CURRIED DEVILED EGGS

BOILED EGGS, SLICED AND YOLKS REMOVED

MAYONNAISE

CURRY POWDER

SALT AND PEPPER

CHUTNEY

Mash the yolks and mix in mayonnaise to a smooth consistency. Sprinkle a little curry powder on the mashed yolks, mix well, taste and add more to taste if needed. Add salt and pepper to taste. Stuff the egg whites. Garnish with a tiny dab of chutney.

SMOKED PAPRIKA DEVILED EGGS

BOILED EGGS, SLICED AND YOLKS REMOVED

MAYONNAISE

SMOKED PAPRIKA POWDER

SALT AND PEPPER

SLIVERS OF SMOKED SALMON, OR PROSCIUTTO, OR HAM

Mash the yolks and mix in mayonnaise to a smooth consistency. Sprinkle a little smoked paprika powder on the mashed yolks, mix well, taste, and add more to taste if needed. Add salt and pepper to taste. Stuff the egg whites. Garnish with slivers of smoked salmon, prosciutto, or ham.

. . .

Stacked Hot Dogs

You can serve these in a roll or on a plate. You'll need really good, homemade mashed potatoes, and a hearty chili, meaty and/or beany, homemade if you can, canned if you must. Get bun length hot dogs, and sturdy rolls, like sub rolls. Cheese on top is optional. Or not.

Toast the rolls. Grill the hot dogs, put them in the rolls, and add a smear of mashed potatoes, then a handsome spoonful of chili right down the length of the dog. You'll see you don't need an awful lot of potatoes or chili, because otherwise you couldn't pick it up without making a mess.

If you can't live without ketchup or mustard on hot dogs, make sure you adorn the dog with them right before you add the mashed potatoes.

A knife and fork version of stuffed hot dog comes from my island neighbor Wendy Hammett who learned from her Grammie. To make Grammie Dogs, she splits the hot dogs lengthwise, then adds mashed potatoes; then grated cheese on top of that, and heats them so the cheese melts. Served on a plate, it makes a homemade fast food.

FOURTH OF JULY CAKE

Shades of Martha Stewart. The idea for a simple sheet cake decorated like the American flag was first described to me by an older island resident long ago. It needs no recipe, just a sheet cake of your choice, iced with white frosting.

Acquire a pint or more of fresh blueberries—the larger high bush sort, and a batch of fresh strawberries. In the upper left-hand corner, set the blueberries on the frosting making a field of blue with white frosting showing through. Then over the rest of the cake, make bands of strawberries alternating with bands of white frosting.

Even if your cake is round, any cake frosted in white with blueberries and strawberries will look like the Fourth of July.

⇒⇒⇒ THANKSGIVING ⇚⇚⇚

Thanksgiving favors cooking massive amounts of food for all the people who gather, whether family who are more likely to travel on this holiday than any other in the year, or all the folks who attend Friendsgiving.

Between Halloween and Black Friday, so much ink is spilled on Thanksgiving in newspapers, magazines, and online that instructions for roasting turkey or making mashed potatoes aren't needed here. A few ideas for soup, sides, relishes, and holiday breads, on the other hand, might be welcome. Then there are leftovers!

CURRIED PUMPKIN BISQUE

This recipe came from my friend Kathleen Curtin with whom I co-authored a book called *Giving Thanks: Thanksgiving History and Food from Pilgrims to Pumpkin Pie*. In my opinion, this recipe is the best in the whole book, a little fussy, but worth the effort.

2 TABLESPOONS BUTTER

1 CUP DICED ONION

1 CUP CHOPPED CELERY

1 CUP PEELED AND CHOPPED CARROT

2 CLOVES GARLIC MINCED

¾ CUPS CANNED, CRUSHED TOMATOES AND JUICE

1 QUART CHICKEN OR VEGETABLE BROTH

1 15-OUNCE CAN PUMPKIN PUREE OR 2 CUPS HOMEMADE PUREE

1 TEASPOON CURRY POWDER, OR MORE TO TASTE

2 BAY LEAVES

1 CUP LIGHT CREAM

SALT AND PEPPER TO TASTE

Melt the butter in a large pot over medium-high heat, add the onion, celery, carrots, and garlic and sauté until the vegetables are very soft, about ten minutes. Then stir in the tomatoes, broth, pumpkin, curry powder, and bay leaves. Bring to a boil, then reduce the heat and simmer for about fifteen minutes. Pick out the bay leaves, and either let the soup cool enough to put into the food processor, or use an immersion blender, and puree all the ingredients together. Add the cream and reheat but do not allow it to boil. Sample and add salt and pepper, and more curry powder to taste. Serve. *{Serves 6 to 8}*

. . .

Chocolate Date Nut Bread

Christine Hessert of Bangor kindly supplied this recipe that came to her from an elderly aunt thirty to forty years ago. She makes it for Thanksgiving along with several other breads, since her holiday has thirty-five to fifty in attendance!

Plain slices of this chocolaty bread are lovely alone with tea or you can make richly sweet tea sandwiches by spreading slices with a cream cheese frosting. Or turn a slice into dessert by putting a scoop of ice cream on a slab of the bread, adding a squirt of whipped cream or a dribble of chocolate sauce on top of that.

1 CUP OF BOILING WATER

2 OUNCES OF CHOCOLATE

1 CUP PITTED CHOPPED DATES

1 CUP SUGAR

¼ CUP BUTTER OR SHORTENING

1 EGG

1 TEASPOON VANILLA

2 CUPS SIFTED FLOUR

2 TABLESPOONS BAKING COCOA (OPTIONAL)

1 TEASPOON BAKING POWDER

½ TEASPOON SALT

½ CUP CHOPPED WALNUTS OR PECANS

Heat the oven to 350 and grease a nine-by-five-inch loaf pan (or two smaller ones). Break the chocolate squares coarsely with a heavy knife and put the chocolate and dates into a bowl and pour the boiling water over them. Let stand until the chocolate is melted and the combination has cooled somewhat. Cream together the sugar and butter, beat in the egg and vanilla. Sift together the dry ingredients and add them to the butter and sugar mixture alternately with the date and chocolate mixture, beating well after each addition. Fold in the nuts. Pour into the loaf pan and bake for an hour or slightly more, until a tester inserted comes out clean. Allow to cool for about ten minutes, then turn it out of the pan to finish cooling. {*Yields 1 nine-by-five-inch loaf*}

• • •

ARTICHOKE MASHED POTATOES

Marinated artichokes in oil are handy to toss into salads, mix into pasta dishes, add to tuna salad sandwiches, or tuck into an omelet. Added to mashed potatoes, they turn the dish into something elegant.

You can certainly use artichokes canned in water; just drain them well.

4 LARGE POTATOES

1 CUP ARTICHOKE HEARTS

{ADVICE}

« *Use pre-chopped dates that you can obtain in the baking section, or a bag of pitted dates labeled "baking dates," found near figs in the fruit and vegetable department of grocery stores. Chopping them up isn't too tedious a chore even though they are a bit sticky. The pre-chopped ones of course are terribly convenient, because you can just dump them into a measuring cup; of course, you pay for the convenience and, in the case of dates, the manufacturers add dextrose to prevent clumping.*

Jack up the bread's chocolate content by adding a couple of tablespoons of dry cocoa to the dry ingredients. Use sweet, semi-sweet, or unsweetened chocolate squares depending on your taste. The bread might even bear the addition of a few chocolate chips along with the nuts.

1 TO 2 CLOVES GARLIC OPTIONAL, PUREED

½ CUP WARM MILK OR CREAM

BUTTER TO TASTE

SALT AND PEPPER

Peel and boil the potatoes until they are tender. Drain. Put the drained potatoes back in the pot and add the artichokes, garlic, and milk and mash thoroughly. Taste, add butter, salt and pepper to taste.

. . .

Winter Squash Wrinkles

I grow butternut squash and, once in a while, buttercups, Hubbards, or kabochas, as well as acorns and delicatas. The butternuts are probably my favorites. If you don't grow them yourself, they are easy to find in the store, at farmer's markets, or farm stands. They sometimes come peeled and cut up, both fresh and frozen.

At Thanksgiving, instead of merely boiling or steaming squash, try roasting it. Heat the oven to 400 degrees, cube the squash, dribble with olive oil and toss until there is a little sheen on the cubes, add minced garlic or not, and roast for fifteen to twenty minutes or until the squash has a little golden color and is fork tender. Cumin is a great addition to squash, and so is a little sprinkle of chili powder.

Another way is to peel and chop up the squash, merely boil it until tender, drain, reserving just about a cup or so of the liquid. Put a handful of dried cranberries in a small dish and pour the liquid over them to soften them for about five minutes, then drain them. Mash the squash, adding butter and maple syrup or brown sugar to taste, then drain and toss in the cranberries, and mix them in. When you are ready to serve the squash, put it into a pretty serving dish and sprinkle some toasted sunflower or pumpkins seeds over the top. It is pretty, tastes good, and is easy-going to put together.

Maine Cranberries

*T*he good news is you can buy cranberries grown in Maine. Whether you live Down East or in Waldo County, there are local cranberry growers: Lincolnville, Dennysville, Columbia Falls, Holden, and Princeton, as well as some closer to Augusta. If you live in one of these towns or next door to one, consider getting some local berries. If you don't see any at the store, ask for them, or look for a farmer's market. Sometimes food co-ops carry them. The heck with the ones from New Jersey or Wisconsin, of all places.

. . .

CRANBERRY RELISH

It wouldn't be Thanksgiving without cranberry sauce or relish.

This easy, peasy relish recipe came from my neighbor, the late Midge Welldon, who got it from her daughter-in-law, Norma Jean. The spices and brandy give it a different character than the usual cranberry and orange or apple relish. The peach brandy in the recipe is the Secret Ingredient, but you can leave it out and still have a good relish. If you don't have peach brandy, just use plain brandy.

. . .

NORMA JEAN'S CRANBERRY RELISH

12 OUNCES OF WHOLE CRANBERRIES (ABOUT 3 CUPS)

1 APPLE, PARED AND CORED, PEELED OPTIONAL

1 CUP OF SUGAR

1 8½-OUNCE CAN CRUSHED PINEAPPLE, WELL
    DRAINED (ABOUT 1 CUP)

½ TEASPOON CINNAMON

¼ TEASPOON CLOVES

¼ TEASPOON GROUND GINGER

4 TABLESPOONS OF PEACH BRANDY

Chop the cranberries and apples in a food processor or run it through a food grinder with a coarse blade. Add all the rest of the ingredients and mix well. Spoon into a container to chill overnight. *{Yields 3 cups}*

• • •

CRANBERRY ORANGE RELISH

I recall when I was a child how much fun it was to operate the grinder that my mom clamped to the edge of the kitchen counter as she filled it with cranberries or orange chunks for the relish. Lots of folks replaced those grinders with food processors, but if you still have one and any children or grandchildren around, chances are good that they will enjoy cranking their way through several cups of relish. It is so simple to make that you could easily add this relish to the table along with jellied cranberry sauce. It's pretty, too.

2 CUPS OF FRESH CRANBERRIES
1 ORANGE, QUARTERED AND SEEDED
1 CUP SUGAR

Run the berries and orange quarters through a food grinder using the medium blade, or process in a food processor until you have a medium coarse texture. Be careful not to make it too fine. Stir in the sugar. Chill in the fridge overnight. *{Yields 3 cups}*

• • •

MARLBOROUGH PUDDING PIE

Forty years ago, when I first became interested in Thanksgiving's food history, I bumped into this lovely version of apple pie. Named pudding, it's baked in a pastry-lined pan as many so-called puddings were in the 1700s. The combination of lemon, cream, and sherry is typically an eighteenth-century flavor profile.

Be sure to use unsweetened applesauce, perhaps homemade if you are up for it. You can get away with all-purpose cream, though heavy is better. Then, in the department of Gilding the Lily, you can also serve it with whipped cream on top.

½ CUP SUGAR

6 TABLESPOONS (¾ STICK) BUTTER, MELTED

4 LARGE EGGS, WELL-BEATEN

½ CUP HEAVY CREAM

1 LEMON

1 CUP UNSWEETENED APPLESAUCE

½ CUP SWEET OR CREAM SHERRY

½ TEASPOON GRATED NUTMEG (OR TO TASTE)

1 UNBAKED 9-INCH PIE CRUST

Preheat the oven to 350 degrees. In a large bowl, mix well the sugar and butter, then beat in the eggs and the cream. Grate lemon zest (just the yellow part) into the sugar, butter, cream, and eggs, and then squeeze in the juice, straining out the seeds. Add the applesauce, sherry and nutmeg, and pour into a pastry-lined pie plate. Bake about an hour until the filling is set. You can test with a knife or jiggle the plate to see if the center is firm. Cool and serve with whipped cream. *{Makes 1 nine-inch pie}*

⇒⇒⇒ THANKSGIVING ⇐⇐⇐
LEFTOVERS

. . .

Turkey Sandwiches

Lots of us eat Thanksgiving Dinner in the early afternoon on Thursday, scraping up last bits of pie around 3:00 p.m., and then after a nap, more conversations with family and friends, maybe a little football on television, and the inevitable dish-washing. One might feel a little peckish come 7:30 or 8:00 p.m. Perfect time for two pieces of bread spread with mayonnaise, some thinly sliced turkey, a dab of cranberry sauce, and maybe even some stuffing, even slicing it and toasting it on a griddle before sandwich assembly.

Hot turkey sandwiches are wonderful, too. This time, heat up the gravy and put the bread, toasted, on a plate, pile on the turkey, and slather it with gravy, and have cranberry sauce on the side.

Towards a Calm Thanksgiving

If you don't cook from scratch, or if your dinners routinely come from the prepared-food section of grocery store freezers, then I could understand why making Thanksgiving dinner for your family or a crowd might be a scary proposition. Each year, I note the angst and anxiety underlying the pre-Thanksgiving writings of big city newspapers, blogs, and the November issues of food magazines and I think, Thanksgiving is no time to get in a pucker. A traditional holiday dinner is one of the easiest and comfort-food-filled menus we have in our culture. Take a deep breath, just enjoy your family and friends, and save the fancy culinary didoes for show-off dinner parties some other time.

If, however, the deep breath doesn't work, consider the following.

Make it a planned potluck. Ask cousins or siblings or friends to bring mashed potatoes, roasted squash, or creamed onions, or a pie. You take charge of the turkey and stuffing.

Get yourself invited somewhere, and *you* bring the mashed potatoes.

Take advantage of shortcuts: it is more important to enjoy your gathering than peel your own squash. Lots of organizations hold pie sales as fundraisers, and this is a good time to support them and give yourself a break, especially if you can't take the day off before the big holiday to make pies.

The Internet is full of pre-planning and preparation suggestions. Take some time the week before Thanksgiving to peruse a few of them, and make a schedule of your own. Some pies can be baked ahead and frozen, or assembled and frozen for baking on Wednesday before the holiday. Some vegetables can be prepped and stashed in the fridge a couple days ahead. Keep it simple and you'll be just fine.

• • •

Hot Turkey Dishes

Warm up mashed potatoes and serve them with warm turkey slices and gravy. Or use sliced and fried stuffing patties under the turkey and gravy.

Leftover pieces of light and dark turkey meat with gravy, baked for a half hour at 350 degrees in a casserole with leftover, or freshly-made, stuffing on top, is really delicious. Don't forget the cranberry sauce.

Turkey shepherd's pie makes a dinner with turkey bits and pieces mixed with gravy, enhanced, if you wish, with onion, peas, leftover green beans, and topped with a layer of mashed potatoes, baked until it is all bubbly. Or turn it into turkey pot pie by topping with pie crust and baking it.

Some people like turkey tetrazzini with pasta and mushrooms. Or turkey à la king with peas over mashed potatoes, or toast, or served in puff pastry shells.

Most of these dishes call for the leftover gravy and when you run out of gravy, you can make sauce with flour, butter, and turkey stock.

If you are a tortilla fan, you can make quesadillas with leftover sliced turkey, cranberry sauce, and jack or cheddar cheese. Cranberry sauce can stand a little capsicum heat with the addition of some chopped jalapenos, or hot sauce.

Turkey salad, too, with raw celery, chopped shallots, mayonnaise, and a sprinkle of dried cranberries served on a bed of lettuce makes a fine lunch.

When you have used up the meat on the bird, then you have this big, gorgeous pile of bones with fragments of turkey attached that you can make into soup. My favorite form of turkey soup has lots of onions and celery in it, and no carrots, and rice, orzo, or barley added to make it.

. . .

Turkey Casserole

4 CUPS OF COOKED TURKEY, LIGHT AND DARK MEAT, CUT INTO
    BITE-SIZED SIZED PIECES
OPTIONAL VEGETABLES, LIKE CORN, PEAS, CARROTS, OR GREEN BEANS
2 CUPS OF TURKEY GRAVY OR SAUCE
2 TO 3 CUPS OF LEFTOVER OR FRESHLY MADE STUFFING

Heat the oven to 350. Grease lightly a two-quart casserole. Spread the turkey meat in the casserole, add vegetables if you wish, and pour the gravy or sauce over the top. Spread the stuffing over the top of that. If you wish, dot the top with bits of butter. Bake for 30 minutes or until the gravy is bubbling and the stuffing is toasted golden. {Serves 4}

CHRISTMAS

...

Swedish Meatballs

Swedish meatballs are a handy item to serve for supper on Christmas Eve or for hors d'oeuvres at the holidays or any other time. Allspice and nutmeg seasoning and the creamy sauce they are smothered in distinguish them from other meatballs. If you prefer not to stand around frying meatballs, Swedish or any other kind, try spreading them in a baking pan and popping them into the oven to brown up. Be sure to scrape up all the browned bits with cooking juices with which you'll make a rich gravy.

You can buy hamburger and ground pork separately, or you can use a meatloaf mix often available in grocery store meat departments. You can also use ground turkey instead of pork.

This is a classic cook-ahead and let stand dish because the meat balls are better the next day.

OLIVE OIL

½ TABLESPOON BUTTER

1 SMALL ONION, DICED

¾ POUND GROUND BEEF

¼ POUND GROUND PORK

2 EGGS, SLIGHTLY BEATEN

1½ CUPS SLIGHTLY DRY BREADCRUMBS

¾ CUP WARM MILK OR CREAM

2 TEASPOONS SALT

½ TEASPOONS PEPPER

¼ TEASPOONS ALLSPICE

¼ TEASPOONS NUTMEG

2 TO 3 TABLESPOONS PAN DRIPPINGS

2 TO 3 TABLESPOONS FLOUR

1 CUP MILK

SALT AND PEPPER TO TASTE

Put a dribble of olive oil together with the butter in a sauté pan and cook the onions until they are just soft, about five minutes.

Put the beef, pork, eggs, crumbs, and evaporated milk or cream into a medium bowl and add the onions, the salt and pepper, and the spices. Mix thoroughly. Form the mixture into balls about an inch or two in diameter, and fry over a medium heat, turning them as each side browns, until they are all done. Remove to another cook pan or a casserole. Drain all but about two to three tablespoons of the pan drippings from the fry pan then add two to three tablespoons of flour to the pan and cook, whisking to blend. Slowly pour a cup of milk, or more if needed, into the pan, whisking to make a smooth gravy and cook until it thickens, and add salt and pepper to taste. Pour over the meatballs in a casserole dish. Hold for a day and rewarm in a moderate 350-degree oven to serve. *{Makes about 4 to 5 servings as a main dish}*

. . .

Fruitcake Really Worth Making

Fruitcake has ended up the butt of jokes and ridicule. Truthfully, some of it is deserved. Too many fruitcakes found in stores are made with that awful dyed citrus peel and goodness knows what else. Homemade fruitcakes with raisins, nuts, genuine citron, and preserved lemon and orange peels, then drenched in brandy and carefully aged is wonderful stuff and hearkens back to an earlier time when such things were an occasional treat.

So, just to show how good a fruit-laden cake can be, here is the Fruitcake Hater's Fruitcake, a recipe from my island neighbor Cynthia Rosenberger who gave loaves to friends at Christmas.

This cake is in the white fruitcake, or perhaps more aptly, golden fruitcake tradition. Lovely morsels of dried apricot, sugary dates, plump golden raisins, and rich pecans embedded in a buttery batter enriched with juice and cream, and gently spiced, form the cake, the perfect and wholesome addition to a tray of Christmas cookies, and then ideal for an accompaniment to tea some cold January afternoon, or even to cheer us up in mud season, if there is any left.

Cynthia found this recipe, developed by Gene Cedarholm, in a 1977 *Gourmet* magazine. It makes four large loaf pans full, but I decided to halve the recipe, and bake three in small loaf pans as gifts for holiday consumption and keep one larger one for us.

Normally, I don't keep apricot nectar around, so substituted sweet apple cider. The brandy or Cognac and orange liqueur dribbled on top helps to preserve the cake.

The recipe is long, but don't let it seem daunting. Prep all the fruit and nuts. Assemble the dry ingredients. Deal with the butter, sugar, and eggs just as you would for any cake. Half of the dry ingredients are essentially used to dredge the fruit and nuts, but aside from that it all goes together straightforwardly.

Even if you think you have given up on fruitcake, try this one. If you don't like it, then we'll excuse you from future fruitcake.

> 3 POUNDS DRIED APRICOTS, SLICED
>
> 1½ POUNDS PITTED DATES, SLICED
>
> 2 LBS. PECAN PIECES OR HALVES
>
> 1 POUND GOLDEN RAISINS
>
> 2 CUPS (4 STICKS) SOFTENED BUTTER
>
> 2¼ CUPS FIRMLY PACKED LIGHT BROWN SUGAR
>
> 1 CUP HONEY
>
> 10 EGGS
>
> 4 CUPS SIFTED FLOUR
>
> 2 TEASPOONS CINNAMON
>
> 1 TEASPOON GROUND ALLSPICE
>
> 2 TEASPOONS BAKING POWDER
>
> ¾ TEASPOONS SALT
>
> 1 CUP APRICOT NECTAR
>
> ½ CUP LIGHT CREAM
>
> 2 TABLESPOONS LEMON JUICE

LIQUID TOPPING:

> 1 CUP BRANDY OR COGNAC
>
> ¼ CUP ORANGE-FLAVORED LIQUEUR

Heat the oven to 250 degrees. Butter and flour four nine-and-a-half-inch loaf pans. Assemble the fruits and nuts in a large bowl. In another large bowl, cream together butter, brown sugar, and honey. Add eggs, beating well after each addition. In another bowl, sift together flour, spices, salt, and baking powder. Beat half this mixture into the sugar mixture. Add the remaining flour mixture to the fruit and nuts. In a small bowl, combine the apricot nectar, cream, lemon juice, add this to the batter and mix. Finally, fold the dried fruit and nut mix into the batter. Divide the batter among the loaf pans. Bake for two-and-a-half to three hours or until a cake tester inserted in the center comes out clean. Transfer the cakes to racks and let them cool in the pans. Combine the brandy and liqueur and sprinkle each cake with a quarter of the mixture. then let cakes stand at least one hour. Remove cakes from pans and chill them, tightly wrapped in foil, for at least one week.

· · ·

Traditional Plum Pudding

Christmas puddings are much better if you make them well in advance of the holiday—say October or early November, though you can get away with making them in early December.

The full recipe produces two generously sized puddings, about four pounds. You can halve it, however. Feel free to use more generous amounts of spice. I generally double the spice. If you use dry bread crumbs, use the entire cup of milk; if you use fresh bread crumbs add only enough milk to make a stuff batter.

A tin pudding mold with a lid is perfect for steaming. Muslin-covered pudding bowls work very well: cut the cloth so it covers the bowl generously and have string ready to tie it on. Heat a deep roasting pan of water to put the puddings in as soon as they are mixed and keep a kettle of hot water ready to add more water to it as it steams away. You can put the roasting pan and puddings in the oven at 350 degrees, too, if you don't want to do it on the top of the stove.

To serve the plum pudding, I warm it in a steamer or wrap it in tin foil in the oven. Be sure to flame it with more rum or brandy. Turn out the lights, and take it to the dinner table with blue fire flickering around it. Spectacular. Serve hard sauce alongside, which will turn sweetly creamy on the warm pudding.

3 CUPS FLOUR

3 CUPS BREADCRUMBS

3 CUPS SUGAR

3 CUPS RAISINS

3 CUPS SUET, GRATED

3 CUPS CURRANTS

3 CUPS GOLDEN RAISINS

4 BEATEN EGGS

ZEST OF 2 LEMONS WITH JUICE OF 1 LEMON

½ POUND OF MIXED CANDIED PEEL

2 TEASPOONS BAKING POWDER

1 TEASPOON SALT

1 TEASPOON BAKING SODA

1 TEASPOON NUTMEG

1 TEASPOON CINNAMON

1 TEASPOON ALLSPICE

1 PINT RUM

1 CUP MILK (LESS IF YOU USE FRESH BREADCRUMBS)

Grease and flour the pudding molds or bowls you will use for steaming and heat water for steaming. Mix together in a large bowl the flour, crumbs, sugar, raisins, suet, currants, and golden raisins. Then add in eggs, lemon juice peel, baking powder, salt and all spices. Add the rum, and gradually the milk, stirring until you have a stiff batter. Distribute among molds or bowls, filling each two-thirds full. Dip the cloth in hot water, then tie it over the top of the bowls, a little puckered so there is room to swell. Place in pans with hot water half-way up molds. Steam for an hour, checking small ones after an hour, and allowing larger ones another half hour. They will look like a damp cake, and a skewer inserted will come out clean. When they are done, take them from the pans, and when cool enough to handle turn out on racks. Wrap puddings in the cloth you tied over the bowls, or in muslin, and put them in a large container (I use my enamel canner) and douse them generously with rum. Keep for months, but check occasionally, and add more rum to keep them damp and sticky. {*Makes 4 pounds of pudding*}

Magic Numbers for Traditional Pudding

*T*his magical recipe comes from my island neighbor Sharon Daley's husband Tom's family. Tom is descended from a Cornish family from near Penzance, England. His Cornish grandmother, Mabel Hocking, made this pudding at Christmas time, even after the family came to Boston in the 1920s.

Tom remembers Nana making the puddings in big earthenware bowls. The puds sat, magnificent and mysterious, covered with cheese cloth, on the top shelf of her pantry. As a child, Tom and his cousins ate their servings warm with sugar sprinkled on them, though the grown-ups had theirs with more rum dribbled on them.

· · ·

Italian-Style Anisette Cookies

Anyone who enjoys licorice flavors will appreciate these slightly cakey anisette cookies topped with a little anise-flavored frosting.

Don't let them brown. They are meant to be soft, so once the tops are barely firm—test by putting your finger on them—pull them out of the oven. It's okay if the bottoms are lightly golden.

Cookies:

    4 CUPS ALL-PURPOSE FLOUR

    1 CUP WHITE SUGAR

    1 TABLESPOON BAKING POWDER

    ¾ CUP VEGETABLE OIL

    ½ CUP MILK

    2 LARGE EGGS

    1 TO 2 TABLESPOONS ANISE EXTRACT

Icing:

    1 CUP CONFECTIONERS' SUGAR

    2 TABLESPOONS HOT MILK

    2 TO 3 TEASPOONS ANISE EXTRACT

{ADVICE}

≪ *Clearly anise is not an important flavoring for Yankees. I found it a little difficult to find anise extract in larger than one-ounce bottles and I easily used up the whole bottle in order to get the strength of anise flavor I prefer. Ordering from an online source can sometimes yield you a larger amount. Professional bakers might use a food-grade anise oil by the drop, but that is hard to find as well. Further boost the anise flavor by adding extract to the frosting.*

Heat the oven to 375 degrees. Grease cookie sheets or line them with parchment paper. In a large bowl, whisk together the flour, sugar, and baking powder. Form a well in the center and pour in the oil, milk, eggs, and anise extract. Stir all together to make the dough. Roll dough into balls, flatten slightly, and put them on the cookie sheets. Bake until the tops are still pale and are just firm, about twelve minutes. To make the icing, mix confectioners' sugar, hot milk, and anise extract together until smooth. Dip the cookie tops into the icing, then sprinkle on decorations if desired and allow to cool. {Makes 25 cookies}

. . .

PECAN SNOWBALL COOKIES

1 CUP BUTTER

¾ CUP CONFECTIONERS' SUGAR

2½ CUPS FLOUR

1 TEASPOON VANILLA

1 CUP FINELY CHOPPED PECANS

ADDITIONAL CONFECTIONER'S SUGAR FOR ROLLING

Heat the oven to 375 degrees and line a cookie sheet with parchment paper. Cream together the butter and confectioners' sugar. Add all the rest of the ingredients and mix well enough to make a dough firm enough to form balls. Roll small balls in your hands and place on ungreased cookie sheet. Bake for twelve to fifteen minutes, or until light brown, checking after ten minutes. Cool completely and roll in confectioners' sugar. {Makes 3 dozen}

. . .

CHEWY NOELS

This recipe from Kay Grover in Sedgewick makes the fastest cookie bar in Down East Maine. She wrote, "Because while the recipe sounds a bit weird, they really are delicious and very quick and easy to make when something is needed for tea or coffee." Don't, however, file these with Christmas-only cookies, because they could be Chewy Hearts for Valentines, or Chewy Fourths for Independence Day, or Any-Purpose Chewies for all the rest of the time.

Lost and Found Recipes

"Some years ago," Kay Grover of Sedgewick wrote, "I asked you if you had a recipe for Chewy Noels. While looking for a different recipe, I finally found mine."

Ah, who can't relate to that? I don't know about you, but I have a few piles, and file folders, and a box or two stuffed with recipes I think I will try someday; tried once and meant to put into a notebook; or want to think about some more before I toss them out. It's the ones I tried and liked and can't find again that drive me the most nuts.

Of course, young people, and a select group of my peers, too, just take pictures of recipes with their ever-present smart phones to store electronically. Something to be said for that.

Also, this recipe translates neatly and deliciously into a treat for the gluten-avoiders in our midst. Use all-purpose, so-called gluten–free replacement flour, easily located these days in the baking aisle, and you are in business. For the chopped nuts, choose slightly fattier ones like walnuts or pecans.

To decorate, dust with confectioners' sugar, or as Kay suggested, "If you want to be fancy you can write Noel across each bar with any kind of frosting."

2 TABLESPOONS BUTTER

2 EGGS

1 CUP LIGHT BROWN SUGAR, PACKED

5 TABLESPOONS ALL-PURPOSE FLOUR OR GLUTEN-FREE FLOUR

⅛ TEASPOON BAKING SODA

1 CUP CHOPPED NUTS

1 TEASPOON VANILLA

CONFECTIONERS' SUGAR

Preheat oven to 350 degrees. Melt the butter in a nine-by-nine baking pan over low heat and swirl it to spread the butter to all corners. Beat the eggs slightly. In a separate bowl, combine the sugar, flour, soda, and nuts, then add them to the eggs. Pour the mixture gently over the butter but do not stir. Bake for twenty minutes. Take out of oven, and let cool briefly, then cut into bars and cool on a rack. When they are cold, dust with confectioner's sugar.

. . .

Chocolate Peanut Crunch Clusters

This recipe for a peanut and chocolate candy sent along by a reader who wrote about the clusters, "Rave reviews!! (go figure) The girls at my bank and doggie day care loved them." She decided to make them for neighbors next. Lucky neighbors.

Her recipe calls for semi-sweet chocolate morsels and peanut butter plus peanuts. You can tinker a bit here with sweetness if you prefer, by using milk chocolate morsels or dark chocolate, and also by observing whether or not your peanut butter has sweetening in it. Many do; just read the label. For this recipe we prefer the smooth kind that has peanuts and salt in it and nothing else.

    24 OUNCES (ABOUT 4½ CUPS) SEMI-SWEET CHOCOLATE CHIPS
    1 CUP SMOOTH PEANUT BUTTER
    16 OUNCES (ABOUT 3½ CUPS) DRY ROASTED PEANUTS

Melt the chocolate chips in a double boiler or in the microwave and stir in the peanut butter until the mixture is hot and smooth. Add the peanuts and mix to distribute them evenly. Drop by small spoonfuls on waxed or parchment paper lined cookie sheet. Decorate with sprinkles if desired. Refrigerate overnight or all day. Remove from the paper and store in an airtight container until serving. {Makes 10 dozen small clusters}

. . .

Mrs. Willetts Cookies

This recipe came from Mrs. Willetts, who lived in Old Mystic, Connecticut, when I worked at Mystic Seaport, where her husband Howard also worked. At Christmas 1969, my friend and mentor Jane Keener and I made a huge batch of these to serve at a staff party, and I liked them so much that I've made them nearly every Christmas since, over fifty years now. Made only with butter, sugar, and flour, these roll and cut cookies taste like shortbread. They can be a bit crumbly to work with but roll and cut them at room temperature for best results. Icing isn't really the best bet for decorating them. Sprinkles work better.

You may wish to beat an egg until it is frothy and brush the top of cookies with it.

    1 POUND (4 STICKS) BUTTER
    5 CUPS FLOUR
    1 CUP LIGHT BROWN SUGAR

Heat the oven to 375 degrees and grease a cookie sheet or line it with parchment paper. Mix all the ingredients together until it makes a stiff dough. Roll and cut cookies.

. . .

Classic Eggnog

Fanny Farmer's classic recipe for eggnog, a wonderful recipe and very spirited, has been the standard at our house. Plan to make eggnog a week or more ahead of serving time to allow the flavors to develop and meld. The alcohol loses its bite, leaving deep flavor behind. Just keep it cold. Sugar and alcohol are preservatives, and you need not fret about whether it is still good for a week or two, or even more.

The old Farmer recipe calls for a dozen eggs, a quart *each* of milk, heavy cream and bourbon and an additional cup of rum, yielding about a gallon. Leftover eggnog is terrific for making French toast, or adding to pumpkin puree for pie. (The alcohol is cooked out of it by the time the French toast is done and a pie is baked.)

If you have not yet discovered the fragrant blessing of freshly grated nutmeg, this is a good time to give it a try. Use the finest side of a box grater or a microplane to grate it. Often, you can reduce the amount of nutmeg a recipe calls for because it is so pungent when fresh.

Lest you be concerned about uncooked eggs in eggnog, note that the recipe calls for heating the milk or cream so that it cooks the eggs enough, and the alcohol finishes the job.

3 CUPS WHOLE MILK

1 CUP HEAVY CREAM

1 VANILLA BEAN POD, SPLIT TO EXPOSE SEEDS, OR 2 TEASPOONS
    VANILLA EXTRACT

1 TEASPOON NUTMEG, PLUS MORE FOR GARNISH

5 LARGE EGGS, SEPARATED

½ TO ⅔ CUP GRANULATED SUGAR

1 CUP DARK RUM AND/OR BOURBON, WITH MORE TO TASTE

In a heavy-bottomed saucepan, combine milk, cream, vanilla bean and seeds, and nutmeg. Stirring only occasionally, bring the mixture just to a boil over a medium heat, then remove from the heat for about five minutes. In a large bowl, beat egg yolks and sugar until they form thick ribbons when you lift the beater. Slowly stir in the hot milk, cream, and sugar mixture until it is completely incorporated. Stir in bourbon and/or rum. Refrigerate overnight or for up to a week. Before serving, beat the egg whites until soft peaks form then fold gently into eggnog. Serve with more fresh grated nutmeg. {Makes a quart and a half}

⇒⇒⇒ NEW YEAR ⇐⇐⇐

Appetizers help with entertaining guests not only for the last night of the year, but whenever we want a little something to offer friends pre-dinner or to accompany drinks. Then, too, it's handy to have something to contribute when we are guests.

New Years' meals often have a good luck theme; two dishes below symbolize prosperity and good luck.

• • •

Slam Dunk Cracker Spread

As long as you have a package of cream cheese, a jar of jam, jelly, or chutney, and a box of crackers, you can whip together a fast and tasty appetizer. It doesn't even need to be cream cheese: goat cheese, mascarpone, or some other soft white cheese will do just as well. Put a portion of it on a plate and spoon over it a sweet or savory jam or jelly (like red pepper jelly, garlic or onion jam) or the chutney of your choice. Open a box of crackers and arrange them around the cheese, put out a spreader and relax.

. . .

Hot Jalapeno Bites

Ginny Hall, formerly of Islesboro who now lives in Philadelphia, used to make these for her parties. Very simple to make, you can assemble them in advance and bake them as a hot hors d'oeuvre as needed. Satisfyingly rich, you could serve them as a brunch item with salad.

3 TO 4 CANNED JALAPENO PEPPERS, CHOPPED AND SEEDS REMOVED

1 POUND CHEDDAR CHEESE, GRATED

6 EGGS, BEATEN

Heat the oven to 350 degrees and grease a nine-by-thirteen-inch baking dish. Spread half of the cheese in the baking dish. Sprinkle the chopped peppers over the cheese, then spread the rest of the cheese over the peppers. Pour the beaten eggs over the cheese. Bake for thirty to forty minutes, until the whole has baked solid and the top is lightly golden. Cut into bite-sized pieces.

. . .

Bacon Wrapped Dates

Laurie Littlefield-Baas taught in the Islesboro school and now lives in New Hampshire. She stays in touch and recently sent this good idea for a delicious appetizer. She wrote that she and her husband enthusiastically call them "Bacon candy!!! No added sugar but oh so sweet!"

This is less a recipe than a set of instructions.

"Take a box or package of dates. Remove the pits if they still have them. Replace with pecans!!! Take a pound of bacon (we use no nitrate/as clean as pork can be) and cut the strips in half lengthwise and then in half the other way. Visualize that one strip of bacon will result in four "slices". Wrap those slices around the dates and secure with a toothpick. Bake in a 375 degrees oven for thirty-five to forty minutes on a parchment paper or foil lined cookie sheet." Serve warm.

• • •

Mushroom Roll-Ups

Susan Stucke Funk provided this recipe in 1983 when she, as a newlywed, offered it at a party she and Jim gave for some of us who worked with her at Mystic Seaport. At the time, I was lucky enough to have this bright, energetic woman on my staff; a warm, lovely person, and a fellow knitter.

These roll-ups tasted good forty years ago and they still do. Just make sure you use a pliable bread that will roll flat, then not break up when you roll them with the filling inside.

½ POUND MUSHROOMS, MINCED
¼ CUP OR HALF A STICK OF BUTTER
1 CUP LIGHT CREAM
3 TABLESPOONS FLOUR
¾ TEASPOON SALT
2 TEASPOONS MINCED CHIVES
1 TEASPOON LEMON JUICE
1 LOAF THINLY SLICED BREAD, CRUSTS REMOVED

Heat the oven to 400 degrees and lightly grease a baking pan. Sauté the mushrooms in the butter until they are cooked through, just a few minutes. Add the cream and cook over a medium low heat until mixture is thickened. Add the flour, salt, chives, and lemon juice and mix together. Roll the bread until it's flattened and spread each slice lightly with the mushroom mixture. Roll up each slice, and cut into bite-sized pieces. Place on the baking pan and bake for ten minutes. Serve warm. *{Yields about 3 dozen pieces}*

• • •

Hoppin' John

Down South they say it's good luck to eat Hoppin' John on New Years' Day. If it's prosperity you are looking for, then this will benefit your budget any time you make it because rice and bean combinations are as inexpensive as they are wholesome.

I learned this recipe from Cheryl and the late Jim Jamison, who wrote an admirable cookbook fourteen years ago called *American Home Cooking,* using recipes they collected as they traveled around the country. I have made it several times, even though I am a baked beans and brown bread kind of girl.

1 CUP DRIED BLACK EYED PEAS

1 SMOKED HAM HOCK, OR HAM BONE WITH MEAT ON IT

1 LARGE ONION, CHOPPED

6 CUPS OF WATER

A SPRINKLE OF RED PEPPER FLAKES OR CAYENNE PEPPER,
    OPTIONAL TO TASTE

SALT AND BLACK PEPPER TO TASTE

1 TEASPOON DRIED THYME

1 CUP RICE

HOT SAUCE, OPTIONAL

Put the peas, ham hock, onion, and water in a large, heavy-bottomed cook pot and add the red pepper, salt and black pepper, thyme. Bring to a boil, then lower the heat and simmer for about an hour, or until the peas are tender but haven't broken apart. As soon as they are tender, take the pot off the heat and drain it, reserving two cups of the liquid to add back to the pot. If your ham hock has meat on it, pick the meat off, and cut it into bite-sized pieces and return them to the pot. If you have extra liquid, save it for soup. If you don't have enough, add water. Add the rice, and cook until the rice is done, about twenty to twenty-five minutes. Serve it with the optional hot sauce. {*Serves 4 to 6*}

• • •

$\mathcal{L}$ENTILS FOR $\mathcal{L}$UCK

What do you eat to promote luck in the New Year? Dyed-in-the-wool New Englanders don't have a traditional food to ensure good fortune, possibly because Yankees think that we make our own luck as best we can by industry and thrift.

Some in Europe eat greens because it looks like money, or

pork, because pigs, who root forward, symbolize progress. Italians and French eat a lentil soup because the little lentils are round like coins and swell, which we certainly like money to do.

The recipe for the lentil soup reminded me that a cook can make almost anything taste very good by starting with the basic aromatic vegetables of onion, celery, carrots, and, if you like it, garlic. Add a bay leaf, or rosemary, salt and pepper, maybe a little red pepper. If you want a heartier dish, this soupy stew can handle the addition of a sweet Italian sausage, or some chourizo, or ham. As it stands the recipe works for vegans, vegetarians, and gluten-avoiders. I used some chicken broth in addition to water, which deepens the flavor somewhat.

NEW YEARS' LENTIL SOUP

2½ CUPS OF BROWN LENTILS

2 TABLESPOONS OLIVE OIL

1 ONION, CHOPPED

1 CARROT, CHOPPED

1 RIB CELERY, CHOPPED

2 CLOVES GARLIC

6 CUPS OF WATER OR BROTH

1 BAY LEAF OR STALK OF ROSEMARY

SALT AND PEPPER TO TASTE

Rinse the lentils and soak overnight. Put the olive oil in a soup pot, and add the onion, carrots, celery, and garlic and cook until they are slightly softened. Add the water or broth to the vegetables, and then the soaked lentils and bay leaf. Bring to a boil, then reduce the heat and simmer until the lentils are soft but not mushy. Add salt and pepper to taste and serve. {Serves 6 to 8}

7

HAVE A DRINK

It's true. Maine was the first state in the nation to pass a total ban in 1851 on alcohol. Almost total that is, with exceptions for medicinal, mechanical, and manufacturing purposes. Starting in 1838, Portland's Mayor Neal Dow led the Temperance movement resulting in the 1851 law, with Prohibition starting in 1920, only to be repealed in 1933. There still are a few "dry" towns in mostly rural northern and western Maine.

Now, though, many breweries have sprung up all over the state producing beer and cider; bourbon and whiskey distilleries using locally grown grains; mead from honey; and gin and vodka from our famous potatoes.

Some of us enjoy making cordials and syrups from fruits we grow or gather in a centuries-long tradition of home-produced enhancements to add to bubbly soda, seltzers, champagne, prosecco, or wine and liquor, or to sip after dinner. The following suggestions and recipes for cold and warm potables made with and without spirits give you easy and enjoyable options.

COLD WITHOUT

. . .

Rhubarb Cardamom and Lemon Syrup

This recipe for a spiced sweet syrup enhances seltzer or club soda. Soon-to-be-mothers may enjoy this alternative to soda pop, or other sugary beverage; this tart, slightly spiced mix creates an ideal alternative to an alcoholic beverage.

Then there is the pour-over-ice cream possibility, or add to sorbet mix before freezing, say for a strawberry or lemon sorbet.

If you wish to use this with spirits, consider adding it to a rose wine and seltzer cooler. Refreshing and delicious. Try it in prosecco, too.

1 POUND RHUBARB STALKS, CHOPPED INTO ONE-INCH PIECES

3 TEASPOONS DECORTICATED CARDAMOM SEEDS

2 CUPS SUGAR

2 CUPS WATER

JUICE AND ZEST OF ONE LEMON

Combine in a heavy saucepan the rhubarb, cardamom, and sugar, stirring so that the rhubarb is covered in sugar. Let stand for an hour or two until the sugar is sticky and you can see a little dissolving begin. Add the water and bring to a steady simmer for about twenty to thirty minutes, or until the rhubarb is cooked apart. Add the lemon zest and simmer for another five minutes. Remove from the heat, stir in the lemon juice, and strain through a fine sieve. The syrup will be thin. Taste and adjust for sweetness by adding a little more sugar if desired, returning it to the heat until the sugar is dissolved. Store refrigerated. {Makes 3 cups}

. . .

Watermelon Juice

The watermelon juice idea comes from a YouTube video out of Azerbaijan called "Country Life" featuring an older couple who demonstrate making a great many of their favorite dishes and preserves, not just traditional ones either, on their farm.

A recent episode showed how they turned a big pile of watermelons into bottled juice for year-round use (then preserving the peeled rind in sugar syrup). The woman whacked off the top of the melon and she and her husband used a paint mixer put on a drill adapted to serve as an immersion blender to puree the interior. Scooping out the puree, they strained out the fruit and canned the juice. Intrigued, I decided to try it for myself.

I acquired one of those small seedless watermelons abounding in produce sections. I cut off one end and carved out an inch or so into the melon, then pureed it with my immersion bender. Without one of those, you could simply chop up watermelon chunks to toss into a blender, then strain out the juice. I ended up with slightly less than two quarts.

Delicious as is, you could add vodka or white rum, and perhaps some lime juice to taste if you wanted a cocktail sort of thing.

→→→ COLD WITH ←←←

. . .

RHUBARBARUS GIMLETS

Randy Dorman, who made the Rhubarb Cardamom and Lemon Syrup, used it to concoct what he named a Rhubarbarous Gimlet. He observed that rhubarb syrup has a particular affinity for sour cocktails of all kinds. He wrote, "Cocktails in this family (including classics like whisky sours, margaritas, and daiquiris) are all essentially riffs on a master formula of two parts base liquor to one part citrus and one part sweet. Your syrup is easily swapped in for the sweet element, with the rhubarb adding a little bitter and the cardamom a little spice to complement the basic interplay of sweet and sour.".

I love sweet and sour cocktails; whiskey sour is my winter favorite. Since a gimlet is a gin sour, I was delighted to try this gimlet which was, as Randy said, "Just the thing for a hot July afternoon!"

RANDY DORMAN'S RHUBARBAROUS GIMLET

2 OUNCES GIN

1 OUNCE FRESH LIME JUICE

1 OUNCE RHUBARB, CARDAMOM, AND LEMON SYRUP

Combine ingredients in a cocktail shaker filled with ice. Shake hard until very cold and strain into a chilled coup or cocktail glass.

Rhubarb and Cocktails

andy Dorman reported that cocktail mixing had been a hobby for ten years now. Lots of people have joined in with mixology, and interesting syrups, artisanal mixers, and locally distilled alcohols help add to the fun of experimenting with cocktails.

Island friends Anmiryam Budner and her husband Martin Phillip have also experimented with rhubarb syrup and cocktails. Anmiryam's syrup recipe is very simple: "We chop up a bunch of rhubarb into chunks. Cover with an equal measure or a bit more of water. Add about three-quarters to one cup sugar for every four cups of rhubarb. Boil until the rhubarb is mush. Strain the solids, catching the syrup into a bowl. Done." Her favorite use is for whiskey sours, but they use it in margaritas, too, and sometimes simply with seltzer.

• • •

MINT JULEP

My friends Kathy and Mike Kerr served a perfectly lovely mint julep one evening that, to be truthful, I wasn't completely certain I'd enjoy, having had one several years ago that I did not like well enough to eagerly anticipate the next one. The Kerr's recipe, on the other hand, proved that mint, sugar, and bourbon refreshed deliciously. Mike, the family julep maker, shared his instructions.

"Cut up four largish mint leaves into fifteen to twenty smaller pieces and put into a heat-proof glass. Pour in hot water, which needn't be boiling, enough to wet the leaves plus just a little more; muddle the mixture for four to five minutes to bring out the flavor of the mint. Add at least three to four tablespoons powdered sugar.

Then add two ounces good quality bourbon (or more to your taste; stir the mix well; fill the glass you are making it in with chips of ice (not very small, just large enough to last as you drink); add a stem of mint leaves to the glass that comes enough above the rim of the glass to bury your nose in them as you drink up. Enjoy!"

Enjoy indeed.

• • •

Sangria

Fruit turns wine into a sweet summery drink. You can use white or red wine, depending on the kind of fruit you choose. White wine seems to work best with lemons, limes, oranges, peaches, pears, summer berries like strawberries and raspberries. Red wines also use lemon and oranges, and stand up well to sturdy flavored fruit like plums, blueberries, and blackberries. It's best to sweeten sangria to taste, using your own homemade simple syrup.

You might hear about adding ginger ale which would sweeten it further, or you might opt for club soda if you wanted any fizziness at all. It's perfectly fine without any carbonation.

RED SANGRIA

1 LEMON, SLICED

1 ORANGE, SLICED

1 BOTTLE RED WINE (A RIOJA, PINOT NOIR, MALBEC, SHIRAZ)

SIMPLE SYRUP, TO TASTE

CLUB SODA OR SPRITZER, OPTIONAL

Put the sliced fruit into large pitcher or jar. Add the wine, stir, and let stand for eight hours. Taste and sweeten with simple syrup. Chill and serve garnished with slices of orange or lemon. Add club soda if you wish. Ice cubes are optional.

• • •

Apple Cider

A couple of galvanized washtubs, two or three old bushel baskets, a spackle bucket, and two tall wicker baskets are full of apples out in the barn awaiting grinding and pressing sometime soon for homegrown apple cider. If it's a good apple year, my neighbors Nancy and Terry Wuori and I go out scavenging apples, figuring it's better we rather than the deer clean up under laden trees. Then we gather at their house to press the cider to take home in the jugs and juice containers that we've saved up for a couple of months.

There is always enough to freeze, and lots to drink. I let some get fizzy, which it will do if it isn't pasteurized, and I enjoy the natural carbonation very much.

I drink my cider both hot and cold, plain and with additions. Ginger and apples go very well together, so my favorite add-in is ginger brandy which you can find at better-stocked liquor stores and rarely at supermarkets. Another is allspice dram (see below). Or make Cider Cocktail; the recipe follows.

CIDER COCKTAIL
4 OUNCES SWEET APPLE CIDER
1 OUNCE DARK RUM
½ OUNCE WHISKEY
GINGER BEER

Put a couple ice cubes in a glass, and add the cider, rum and whiskey and stir.

LIQUEURS

• • •

Allspice Dram

The lovely warm flavor of allspice, a spice oddly not as much in fashion with baking these days and which works beautifully in cakes, cookies, and anything made with apples, and as an infusion in white rum, enhances all kinds of beverages. Served hot or cold, put a drop or two in wine, or add it judiciously to other cocktails. One of my favorite winter drinks now is warm cider, a

Homemade Liqueurs and Cordials

*F*itting out a home bar with all the special concoctions that make for interesting and complex cocktails, or supplying ourselves with ingredients for cooking with liqueurs, can cost us a pretty penny. Fortunately, a bottle of inexpensive vodka, light rum, or brandy, and some sugar, and spices or fruits to flavor them with, can give us quite a range of flavored liqueurs.

This is a trick that has been around a long time. One of the first I ever tried making came from a cookbook printed in 1833, *The American Frugal House-wife*, which recommended putting lemon peels, when the juice has been squeezed out, into a wide-mouthed jar of brandy. I've done that for years, and use it as one would lemon extract in baking and in sorbets, anytime I need a little punch of lemon flavor.

dash of rum, and a dribble of allspice dram. The dram is fabulous in hot buttered rum.

The dram requires about three weeks to produce. Crush the allspice by using a mortar and pestle gently with a pressing action, or roll them between two sheets of paper towels with a rolling pin. They do not have to be crushed finely.

¼ CUP WHOLE ALLSPICE

1 CUP LIGHT RUM

2-INCH PIECE OF SOFT CINNAMON STICK

1½ CUPS WATER

⅔ CUP LIGHT BROWN SUGAR OR RAW OR TURBINANDO SUGAR

Crush the berries and put into a quart jar with a lid. Add rum and let stand for four days, shaking the jar daily. On day five, break up the cinnamon stick and add to the jar. Steep for twelve days. Strain through a coffee filter into a quart jar. Mix the hot water and sugar together until the sugar is dissolved, then add to the jar with the rum. Let rest for two days before decanting into a bottle with a tight-fitting cap or cork.

...

Orange Liqueur

Commercial orange liqueurs vary a great deal in intensity and flavor, and the distinctions among various brands depend on the makers' formulas. However, a simple orange cordial can often stand in for the others in cooking and even in flavoring some drinks.

The quality of the orange peel itself makes a difference; and if you can obtain bitter oranges or dried bitter orange peel, they will give you better flavor. Use only the orange-colored zest of the orange; I use a vegetable peeler to do the job.

Consider using brandy instead of, or in addition to, vodka, adding three or four whole cloves, and more or less sugar or simple syrup. When you get to the final stage of the liqueur, add the simple syrup gradually, tasting to make it as sweet as you prefer; I stopped after I added about a cup of simple syrup to two cups of the orange-flavored liquor. The orange liqueur will take about three to four weeks to produce.

ZEST OF FOUR TO SIX ORANGES
VODKA OR BRANDY TO COVER (ABOUT 2 CUPS)
2 TO 3 WHOLE CLOVES
SIMPLE SYRUP (1 CUP OF SUGAR IN 1 CUP OF WATER)

Peel the zest off the oranges (and eat the fruit inside) Put into a quart jar with a lid and cover with vodka or brandy. Let stand, shaking gently daily, for two weeks. Add the cloves, and let stand another week or two. Strain the liquor and add the simple syrup to it, to taste. Let stand another day or two then decant into a bottle with a tight-fitting cap or cork.

...

Limoncello

Limoncello (pronounced "lee-mon-CHELL-oh"), a lemon liqueur, that a friend once described as a "granny drink" because it was easily a homemade beverage, is simply lemon peel soaked in clear alcohol, strained and sweetened. Served in a cordial glass following a meal, it promotes digestion and acts as a fitting conclusion to a dinner with friends. You can blend limoncello with other ingredients in cocktails or use it as you might any other cordial, for instance, making lemon sorbet when a recipe calls for a couple of tablespoons of alcohol, or to flavor panna cotta or cake.

It takes minimal effort to make, requiring mostly six weeks of soaking only the yellow portion of lemon peel in pure, unflavored alcohol, during which you do nothing except shake the jar once in a while. Soaking is followed by merely straining the alcohol and adding simple syrup more or less to taste.

5 LEMONS
2 CUPS GRAIN ALCOHOL OR VODKA
SIMPLE SYRUP

Using a vegetable peeler or very sharp knife, remove the zest from the lemons in long strips. Put them into a pint or slightly larger sized jar with a tight lid. Cover the zest with the grain alcohol or vodka. Let stand for forty days or six weeks. Shake jar occasionally. At the end of the soaking time, strain out the zest and discard. Add simple syrup very gradually, tasting as you do so, until you reach your desired sweetness.

{ADVICE}

≪ Clearly anise is not an Everclear; a neutral grain alcohol with a very high proof is the best choice for soaking the peel. (I used one at 151 proof, or 75.5% alcohol by volume) A decent quality unflavored vodka will do. Make your own simple syrup: equal parts water and sugar heated until the sugar dissolves and cooled before using.

I used a pint-sized wide-mouth canning jar, and filled it loosely packed with lemon peel from about five lemons and covered it with the Everclear. Keep your jar out of the light while it is steeping. Make a note on your calendar of when six weeks is up. Alternatively, you may wish to soak the peel for the traditional and Biblically-inspired forty days—partway between five and six weeks.

To enjoy limoncello, plan to serve it very cold. Put the bottle in the freezer an hour before pouring it into cordial or shot glasses. You can even chill the glasses by filling them with crushed ice, which you discard before pouring the liqueur into them.

⇛⇛ CORDIALS ⇚⇚

• • •

Cordially Yours

Here is a general formula, adaptable to several different kinds of small fruit. Making our own cordials is a good deal easier than one might think. Add to champagne, prosecco, club soda, over ice, or neat. The directions yield house presents or comforting sips all year long.

Making Berries Last

*V*odka plus berries plus sugar equals cordial. If I am too busy for words, the strawberries are ripening and in danger of molding. If it is foggy, the raspberries must be ripe. If the birds are flitting in and out of the garden, the blueberries must be ripe. Oh, wouldn't it be grand if all we had time for in this short, summer season was to wander among the berry bushes picking the fruit at its perfection, making pies, jams, jellies, mousses, or wonderful desserts with berries all over them.

Instead, if I get them picked at all, many eaten out of hand in the garden, about all I can manage some weeks is to heave them into the freezer and hope for better times. Or I can heave them into vodka and wait until autumn to deal with them.

I've made cordials with vodka mostly, or Everclear, but brandy works, too. You don't need to spend a lot of money on them; use an inexpensive alcohol. The formula is elastic so you can make a small quantity or more, as you wish. You can blend fruits, if you wish, for variations on flavor. Over time, I've learned to use just enough sugar to make a cordial with the right cordial consistency, but not so terribly sweet as to make my teeth ache.

SOFT FRUITS SUCH AS STRAWBERRIES, RASPBERRIES, BLACKBERRIES.
VODKA
SUGAR

Put the fruit into a jar, add just enough vodka to cover. Let stand. When the fruit becomes pale or a month or so has passed, drain it, pressing the fruit very lightly to extract the juice and vodka. Measure it and add an equal or slightly less quantity of sugar. Bring the liquid just to a simmer, and stir in the sugar, stirring until the sugar dissolves completely. Bottle.

• • •

Rhubarb Vodka and Cordial

First comes rhubarb vodka, and then with one more step, you can produce cordial. The process needs three to six weeks, so definitely plan ahead for this.

All you do is cut up a few stalks of rhubarb, cover them with vodka, and let them stand in a tightly covered glass jar. Some rhubarb vodka instructions suggest adding lemon zest, a couple of cloves, or even a piece of cinnamon stick to the jar. When it has sat around for anywhere between three to six weeks, you strain out the rhubarb, and pour a bit of vodka into a glass, add some simple syrup to taste, a couple of ice cubes, and, if you want, club soda, or Prosecco, or even white wine, and then go sit in the shade somewhere to enjoy it. Unbelievably easy.

4 TO 5 RHUBARB STALKS

VODKA

A COUPLE OF STRIPS OF LEMON PEEL, OPTIONAL

3 OR 4 WHOLE CLOVES, OPTIONAL

1-INCH PIECE OF STICK CINNAMON, OPTIONAL

Wash and cut the rhubarb into two inch pieces or so and put into a clean glass jar. Pour just enough vodka into the jar to cover the rhubarb. Put the lid on and allow to stand for about three weeks. Sample the vodka, and when it has a pleasant rhubarb flavor, strain out the rhubarb pieces by running through cheese cloth or a clean dish towel. Let it stand longer if it needs stronger flavor. You may use the vodka as is in a mixed drink with soda, lime, or lemon, grapefruit juice or ginger ale. Store in a clean bottle or jar.

• • •

RHUBARB CORDIAL

SIMPLE SYRUP

RHUBARB VODKA

Add simple syrup to the Rhubarb Vodka to taste. Mix well and store in a clean jar. Serve as a cordial in a small glass, or pour over ice. The syrup will be thin. Taste and adjust for sweetness by adding a little more sugar if desired, returning it to the heat until the sugar is dissolved. Store refrigerated. {Makes 3 cups}

• • •

CRANBERRY CORDIAL

I owe this recipe to a mentor of mine, the food writer Helen Witty, whose wonderful book, *Fancy Pantry*, published in 1986, taught me so much about putting up all sorts of elegant comestibles like the ones that are so easy to spend bucket-loads of money on.

This cordial has a slightly orangey flavor added to tart-sweet brilliant cranberries, and a little spicy boost from cloves and allspice. Several growers in Maine, most of them in Washington County, produce cranberries. If you plan the cordial as a gift, using local cranberries certainly makes the beverage special, even unique.

Spend a few moments to assemble the ingredients; let it sit and soak at room temperature for a month, then strain and bottle. Add to your calendar a weekly reminder to "shake the cranberry cordial."

3½ TO 4 CUPS OR 1 12-OUNCE PACKAGE FRESH CRANBERRIES

2 CUPS SUGAR

DRIED PEEL OF ONE CLEMENTINE OR 1½ TABLESPOONS OF
    GRATED ORANGE ZEST

4 WHOLE CLOVES

4 WHOLE ALLSPICE

1 QUART (4 CUPS) PLAIN VODKA OR WHITE RUM

In a food processor, put half of the berries and half of the peel together with one cup of sugar. Chop coarsely by pulsing a few times, and put it into a large clean glass jar.

⟫⟫⟫ HOT WITHOUT ⟪⟪⟪

It doesn't have to be well below zero with the wind howling for a mug of hot chocolate to warm your hands and heart, whether you start from scratch with cocoa and milk, or have a hot chocolate mix.

Here is a from-scratch recipe for hot cocoa. You can customize it, or a prepared hot cocoa mix you buy, by flavoring your mugful with or without spirits. There are several ways to make your own hot cocoa mix, and lots of milk options, too. If you are new to the process, experiment a little and know that you can stock your pantry with ingredients to grab whenever the urge hits for chocolate comfort.

CHOCOLATE: You can use unsweetened powdered chocolate, dark or not, or chocolate bars or chips, from milk to semi-sweet and unsweetened. If you use powder, you'll have to mix it with a little hot water, milk, or coffee to make a paste which you can thin with milk. If you use chips or chocolate bars, figure on melting it in the hot milk, stirring with a whisk. The great thing about using chips or chunks is that you can add more chocolate at the last minute by merely melting it in. Sample your hot cocoa, and if you want more chocolate punch, add the chips and stir.

SUGAR: Plain old granulated sugar is fine. Light brown or turbinado sugar has a richer flavor. Sweetening can also come from the melted chocolate or from sweetened condensed milk, if you use that.

MILK: Use whatever milk you like, whole, two-percent, even evaporated with water added. Condensed milk is good if you don't have enough regular milk, but don't add sugar until you have tasted the hot cocoa. Plant-based milk works. If you want richer cocoa, use half and half or cream or add some of either to milk.

FLAVORINGS: Coffee or peppermint are just two out of lots of opportunities to season cocoa. If you like coffee, use espresso powder, or espresso chocolate chips, instant coffee, decaffeinated if you wish, dissolved in the milk. Crushed candy canes or hard peppermint candies smashed and dissolved in the hot milk while you're heating the cocoa might please the younger ones in your set and those avoiding spirits. Peppermint or rum extracts also provide those flavors without spirits.

ENHANCEMENTS: Whipped cream or marshmallows floating on top of hot chocolate makes a simple mugful pretty special.

• • •

Homemade Cocoa Mix

¾ CUP WHITE SUGAR

½ CUP UNSWEETENED COCOA POWDER

⅛ TEASPOON SALT

Mix all the ingredients together in a bowl. Transfer mix to an airtight container. Put two or more spoonsfuls in a mug and add hot water or enough hot milk to moisten it, stir, then top with more hot milk. Sample and add more of whatever is needed. Add flavoring if you use it.

• • •

Single Mug of Hot Cocoa

2 TO 3 SPOONSFUL OF POWDERED UNSWEETENED COCOA

2 SPOONSFUL WHITE OR LIGHT BROWN SUGAR

2 TABLESPOONS OF HOT WATER, COFFEE, OR HOT MILK

6 TO 8 OUNCES OF MILK, OR HALF-AND-HALF, OR A MIX OF THE TWO

Put the cocoa and sugar in a small pan or into a mug. Add the hot water, coffee, or milk and stir until the dry ingredients are in a paste. Add the milk and heat gently over a low heat until it is steaming, or put the mug in the microwave to heat the milk. Stir. Sample and add more sugar if desired.

• • •

Glogg

People in Nordic countries serve glogg at Christmas time. The following recipe comes from my sister Sally, who lives in Somerville, and who passed it on to her daughter Sarah, who lives with me. This non-alcoholic option, full of flavor and the charm of the version made with wine, is good enough that when Sarah makes it, some of our dinner guests who would normally drink wine prefer it because it tastes so good. By the way, the raisins left behind in the bottom of saucepan are delicious added to bread pudding, or tapioca, or many baked items calling for raisins.

Sarah recommends making this a couple days in advance and keeping it in the fridge before rewarming it to serve. Consider doubling the recipe if you have a crowd.

1 QUART UNSWEETENED RED GRAPE JUICE OR SPARKING RED GRAPE JUICE

2 QUARTS UNSWEETENED WHITE GRAPE JUICE OR

    SPARKLING WHITE GRAPE JUICE

2 TABLESPOONS ANGOSTURA BITTERS

1 TO 2 CUPS RAISINS

PEEL OF 1 ORANGE

12 WHOLE CARDAMOM PODS BRUISED

10 WHOLE CLOVES

2-INCH PIECE FRESH GINGER

STICK OF CINNAMON

½ TO 1 CUP ALMONDS BLANCHED AND PEELED

SELTZER, OPTIONAL

Mix all ingredients, except the seltzer, together, in a heavy bottomed pan, bring to a simmer, and hold at a simmer for about an hour. Serve or refrigerate to allow the glogg to develop flavor. *{Makes 4 servings}*

. . .

Hot Whisky Punch

Prohibitionist Neal Dow probably never turned to *this* medicinal use of hot whisky punch for a cold or cough. If the common cold or flu strikes your household, you or your loved ones might find this little recipe makes you feel better right away. The lemon and honey works well for the sore throat stage, and the whiskey comes recommended for a cough or for a nightcap before bed.

SLICE OF LEMON

SUGAR

1 OUNCE SHOT OF WHISKEY

HOT WATER

Put a slice of lemon in a mug, add a spoonful of sugar, and mash the lemon and sugar together with a spoon until the juice has run out. Add the whiskey and top off with hot water.

The purpose of most spirited additions to hot beverages is to enhance flavor, not to promote tipsiness. Perhaps the simplest way is merely adding some spice, a couple of cloves, or the merest shake of cinnamon, grating of nutmeg, or macerating a slice of lemon with sugar in the bottom of a mug before adding the beverage. I prefer raw sugar for my sweetening, but plain granulated will do the job.

Following are some of my favorite, and very simple, ways to assemble enhanced hot drinks.

. . .

HOT CIDER

Warm the cider to your desired heat, add a shot of rum, spiced or not, or ginger brandy.

. . .

HOT CHOCOLATE

Add coffee brandy or chocolate liquor to the hot chocolate. Mint-lovers might like a shot of Crème de Menthe. Rum, spiced or not, will warm the cockles. Irish Cream liqueur added to hot chocolate is delicious.

. . .

HOT BUTTERED RUM

In a mug, mash together a half-teaspoon of butter with a shake of cinnamon, and a touch of sugar to taste. Add a shot of rum, and top off with hot water.

. . .

HOT WINE PUNCH

Macerate a slice of orange and one clove with a bit of sugar in the bottom of a mug. Fill the mug halfway with red wine, then top off with hot water.

. . .

NEGUS

Macerate a slice of lemon with a bit of sugar in the bottom of a mug. Fill the mug halfway with port wine, add a shot of brandy, and top off with hot water.

8
Doing It Yourself

There are plenty of good reasons for making your own pre-prepared ingredients, not the least of which is that if you keep pantry items like flour, sugar, baking soda, baking powder, a selection of spices, cocoa, vinegar, and oil, your own mixes will be cheaper than packaged products from the store. Plus, you'll avoid a great deal of packaging, too much of which is plastic and, best of all, you know exactly what foodstuff goes into your mix.

If, on the other hand, you live in an apartment with scant storage space, cook for only one or two people, and can't manage to use up all of an ingredient before it spoils or degrades, then buying pre-prepared ingredients is the most economical thing to do.

Plentiful pantry supplies aren't created in a day. If you need to watch your grocery bill, add one item each time you go to the store: a ten-pound bag of flour one week, baking powder and baking soda the next, and so on. Buy only the spices you like and use, buy larger jars of your favorites; if you don't use allspice very much, just a small jar will last a long time, but if cinnamon sees a lot of play in your house, then a large jar is the way to go.

Of course, your daily schedule will affect how you stock your pantry. Canned beans like kidney or cannellini appear often in recipes as a pantry staple. Of course, dried beans are cheaper, and require overnight or several hours of soaking followed by cooking. Unless you are a relentless plan-ahead type, canned beans will make a great deal of sense. Now that more people work from home, on the other hand, using dried beans is more practicable.

HOMEMADE DRY MIXES

Lots of boxed mixes ask you to add to the contents, which are just dry ingredients, only egg, oil, or milk. Give yourself a head start on your baking projects by premixing the dry ingredients of your favorite recipe, and stashing them in a jar labeled with the recipe's name, setting them aside for when you are ready to bake. You may even decide to write down the recipe and tape it to the jar, so you don't have to dig out the cookbook.

. . .

HOMEMADE PANCAKE MIX

Homemade pre-mixes are particularly handy for simple recipes like pancakes. You can use the following recipe for making a homemade pancake mix which needs only egg, oil, and water to mix them.

> 5 CUPS FLOUR
> 1¼ CUPS OF DRY MILK POWDER
> ¼ SUGAR (OPTIONAL)
> 4 TABLESPOONS BAKING POWDER
> 2 TEASPOONS SALT

Whisk all ingredients together and store in a jar.

TO MAKE PANCAKES WITH THE MIX:
> 1 EGG
> ½ CUP WATER
> 1 TABLESPOON VEGETABLE OIL
> 1 CUP PANCAKE MIX

Whisk the egg, water, and oil together. Put the pancake mix into a bowl and add the wet ingredients, mixing with a few strokes just to make a batter. Add a little more water if you prefer a thinner pancake. Drop large spoonsful of batter on a lightly oiled griddle and bake as usual.

. . .

ℋomemade Biscuit ℳix

Prepared biscuit mix is a handy item. You can find variations online that call for vegetable shortening; I prefer all butter. I love butter flavor, and besides I am an old granola and view the trans-fats in the shortening and margarine with suspicion. You can easily double the recipe that follows.

6 CUPS FLOUR
3 TABLESPOONS BAKING POWDER
1 TEASPOON SALT
1 CUP (2 STICKS) BUTTER, MELTED

Whisk the flour, baking powder, and salt together, or put them in a food processor and whirl it around a few times to mix. Add the melted butter and using a mixer, hand mixer, or processor, dribble the melted butter in a thin stream into the dry ingredients until it is all added. Store the mix in a tightly closed container in a cool cupboard or in the refrigerator. Use in any biscuit or pancake recipe calling for quick biscuit mix. *{Makes slightly more than 6 cups of mix}*

⟫⟫⟩ BROTH AND ⟨⟨⟨ CREAM SOUPS

Pet Peeve: I can't stand paying for water added to something that I can add water to myself, provided I am in the vicinity of a water tap. For example, bottled orange juice, made from concentrate. You can buy frozen concentrate and add your own water.

Other examples: Broth or various canned soups used as sauce. It's not a bad idea to have chicken broth around in case you wake some morning colossally unwell, and nothing will do but a hot

>> *I often save potato boiling water and build my broth on that. Jazz it up with some garlic, substitute leeks for the onion, and add some herbs like parsley, marjoram, and savory. Simmer all together fifteen minutes or until the vegetables are tender. (If you want a deeper flavor, oven roast the vegetables in a little olive oil at 350 until the vegetables are slightly browned. You don't have to heat the oven up on purpose to do this, but stick them in alongside some other thing you are baking.) Drain through a sieve, and store it in a jar in the fridge or freeze it in pint quantities.*

cup of chicken broth before you stumble back to bed.

Usually, I make broth and stock myself, the exception being good old tomato soup to have with a grilled cheese sandwich — fast, convenient, supreme comfort food.

Here are some easy and quick money-saving ready-to use homemade conveniences:

$$\cdots$$

Vegetable Broth

2 CUPS OF WATER

1 CARROT, SLICED

1 ONION, CHOPPED

1 STALK CELERY, SLICED

BAY LEAF

SALT AND PEPPER TO TASTE

HERBS TO TASTE

Combine and simmer until vegetables are tender. Strain for use.
{Yields 2 cups broth}

$$\cdots$$

Chicken Broth

Whenever you roast a chicken (or turkey), put the neck and giblets into a heavy saucepan with an onion, a rib of celery, a carrot, and a bay leaf, and simmer it, using some to baste the bird as it roasts. Then use the broth to make gravy in the bottom of the roasting pan. Freeze any leftover broth to use later.

Save the boney carcass of the chicken, and cook it slowly, barely covered with water, until the joints fall apart then strain it, capturing bits of meat for soup. Remember that though you seem to waste the vegetables, their cost is hardly anything compared with the expense of canned or packaged broth. You could always eat them.

PACKAGE OF GIBLETS AND CHICKEN CARCASS

1 CARROT

1 ONION

1 STALK CELERY

BAY LEAF

SALT AND PEPPER

Simmer all these together until the chicken carcass falls apart.
Strain for use or storage. *{Yield is variable}*

· · ·

CREAM SAUCE

This recipe will save you money on canned cream soups and
help you avoid excess sodium. All you need is butter, flour, and
milk or broth. When you want a vegetable sauce, use the vegetable broth above, if chicken, use your own chicken broth, and
so forth. If you make macaroni and cheese using a sauce, make
a cream sauce with milk and grate the cheese of your choice into
it, adding more milk if it becomes too thick.

2 TABLESPOONS BUTTER OR MELTED FAT

2 TABLESPOONS FLOUR

1 CUP BROTH OR MILK

SALT AND PEPPER TO TASTE

Melt the butter in a heavy pan, stir in the flour, and cook until
the flour looks frothy. Whisk in milk or broth, stirring until the
sauce is smooth. *{Yields 1 cup of sauce}*

· · ·

CREAM SOUP SUBSTITUTE MIX

For another bit of homemade convenience, here is mix from the
Extension Service you can make to use whenever you want to
whip up a sauce quickly.

2 CUPS NON-FAT DRY MILK

¾ CUP CORNSTARCH

¼ CUP INSTANT CHICKEN BOUILLON

2 TABLESPOONS DRIED ONION FLAKES
1 TEASPOON DRIED CRUSHED THYME
1 TEASPOON DRIED CRUSHED BASIL
½ TEASPOON PEPPER

Combine and store in a jar with a tight top. To use, mix ⅓ cup dry mixture with 1¼ cup cold water, cook, and stir till thickened. *{Yields 3 cups of mix}*

⟫⟫ DAIRY PRODUCTS ⟪⟪

. . .

Thick Yogurt

The easiest way to produce thick yogurt is to drain standard plain whole or low-fat yogurt in a sieve until it stops dripping clear liquid. Put the thickened yogurt back in the container and use as usual.

Flavored Yogurt to Go

In a rush, sometimes hungry, and wanting something reasonably healthful to eat, we grab a tiny six-ounce container of flavored yogurt for a quick lunch. Costly though convenient, ultimately all those little plastic containers are so wasteful.

Homemade yogurt flavored with homemade jam or chopped fruits to taste, sweetened with sugar, maple syrup, or honey, made portable with small reusable containers, seems smarter. If you like coffee, vanilla, or lemon-flavored yogurts, then instant coffee, vanilla extract, or lemon extract or juice and a bit of grated rind, added to taste stirred into the thick yogurt do the trick. Stir again before eating in case the yogurt separates.

. . .

Homemade Crème Fraiche

Crème fraiche, lovely stuff to use in desserts instead of sweetened whipped cream, can be a tad costly but is simple to make at home. It needs buttermilk, worth keeping on hand because it is useful for so many baking recipes.

1 CUP HEAVY CREAM
2 TABLESPOONS BUTTERMILK

Stir the cream and buttermilk together in a clean bowl. Cover with a clean dishcloth and set it in a warm part of the kitchen. In twelve to sixteen hours, it will be thickened, but pourable. Stir again and keep in the refrigerator until you are ready to use it. *{Makes about a cup}*

. . .

DIY CHEESE SPREAD

Sure, it's handy to open a jar and spread some cheese on a cracker or spoon it into a bowl to serve with raw vegetables and crackers. For the fifteen minutes or so that it takes to make your own, plus the opportunity to season it to your personal taste, a homemade processed cheese spread is the way to go.

Cheddar cheese, cream cheese, mayonnaise, and sour cream are handy to keep on hand. Smoked paprika adds a very subtle smokiness, while chipotle powder provides pleasant warmth. Add cumin or chili powder. Or none of the above. Go the herbal route instead with dill, chives, garlic, and parsley.

Use a food processor to grate the cheese and then do the job of beating everything together.

So easy, so tasty used as a dip with crudités or crackers, or as a sandwich spread.

8 OUNCES OF SHARP CHEDDAR, GRATED
4 OUNCES CREAM CHEESE
⅓ CUP OF MAYONNAISE
⅓ CUP OF SOUR CREAM
2 CLOVES OF GARLIC PUREED WITH GARLIC PRESS
¼ TEASPOON SMOKED PAPRIKA (OR PLAIN PAPRIKA)
¼ TEASPOON CHIPOTLE POWDER
SALT AND PEPPER TO TASTE

Put all ingredients into the bowl of a food processor and process until the mixture is smooth and spreadable. *{Makes a scant 2 cups}*

. . .

HOMEMADE BOURSIN-STYLE CHEESE

This creamy, garlicky, herb-seasoned cheese works, spread on crackers as an appetizer, or in a sandwich with lettuce plus cold meat like beef or ham, or cucumbers or tomatoes, or dropped on a baked potato. Useful and delicious, it can be a little pricey. Consider poaching the garlic cloves in a tiny bit of water, which softens the garlic enough to reduce its sharpness. If you use ricotta instead of butter, your mock boursin will be lighter fare.

Best made a day in advance, the mixture's flavors need time to blend.

16 OUNCES CREAM CHEESE

8 OUNCES (ONE STICK) BUTTER OR 8 OUNCES OF RICOTTA CHEESE

2 CLOVES OF GARLIC, PUREED

2 TEASPOONS MINCED CHIVES

1 TABLESPOON MINCED PARSLEY

½ TEASPOON DRIED DILL

½ TEASPOON BLACK PEPPER

Beat all together, and pack into a container for refrigeration. *{Yields 1½ pounds of cheese}*

. . .

RANCH DRESSING

It's not just for salads anymore. Ranch-flavored potato chips. corn chips, crackers, and veggie chips abound. The dressing is used for dips for crudités, French fries, and chicken wings and tenders. Mississippi Roast calls for Ranch dressing applied to the meat before braising.

As a mayonnaise-based salad dressing, Ranch dressing is easy to make using with store-bought mayonnaise. Mix some and keep it on hand for all kinds of occasions.

½ CUP MAYONNAISE

¾ CUP SOUR CREAM

¾ CUP BUTTERMILK

1 CLOVE GARLIC, CRUSHED

½ TEASPOON ONION POWDER

¼ TEASPOON DRY MUSTARD POWDER

¼ TEASPOON SALT

1 TABLESPOON WHITE WINE VINEGAR

1 TABLESPOON LEMON JUICE

1½ TABLESPOON WORCESTERSHIRE SAUCE

2 TEASPOON CHOPPED PARSLEY

2 TEASPOON CHOPPED CHIVES

2 TEASPOONS CHOPPED DILL

1 CHOPPED SCALLION

Put mayonnaise, sour cream, and buttermilk in a bowl, and whisk together. Stir in garlic, onion, mustard powder, salt, vinegar, lemon juice and Worcestershire sauce. Add parsley, chives, dill, and scallion, stirring to distribute through the sauce. Take a taste to check for salt, adjust as needed. Add more buttermilk or mayonnaise if you want a thinner mixture.

⤠⤠⤠ SPICE BLENDS ⤡⤡⤡

If you cook from scratch a lot, you probably keep a generous number of spices on your shelf. You probably *don't* keep malto-dextrin, silicon dioxide, citric acid, and "natural flavor," whatever that is, among your jars—all items that appear on packets of popular seasoning mixes for everything from spaghetti sauce to chili to tacos.

Let's begin with an all-purpose seasoning salt, suitable for a wide range of cooking purposes.

SEASONING SALT

3 TABLESPOONS TABLE SALT

3 TEASPOONS SUGAR

1¾ TEASPOONS PAPRIKA

1 TEASPOON TURMERIC

1½ TEASPOON ONION POWDER

1 TEASPOON GARLIC POWDER

1½ TEASPOON CORNSTARCH

Sift all the ingredients together into a small bowl. Empty into a small jar, preferably one with a shaker top and screw on lid. {Makes about ⅓ cup}

TACO SEASONING

In an experimental mood once, I mixed up one recipe's worth of taco seasoning from scratch and compared it to the packet seasoning. By golly, they smelled the same to me.

So, here's taco seasoning mix that you can use when you make tacos or taco pie. More red pepper makes the mix snappier; I prefer chipotle powder. Mix it up and stash it away for any time you want a Tex-Mex flavor.

1 TABLESPOON CHILI POWDER

2 TEASPOONS CUMIN

1 TEASPOON GARLIC POWDER

½ TEASPOON ONION POWDER

1 TEASPOON PAPRIKA

¼ TEASPOON SALT

¼ TEASPOON BLACK PEPPER

1 TEASPOON OREGANO

⅛ TO ¼ TEASPOON RED PEPPER FLAKES, TO TASTE

Mix all together in a small bowl and store in a jar.

...

Pumpkin Spice Blend

There's no need to buy pre-mixed pumpkin pie spice when you can measure out cinnamon, ginger, nutmeg, and cloves or allspice. If you like having one jar to reach for when you make a pumpkin pie, bread, cake, frosting or any pumpkin spice flavored item, consider assembling the spices and mixing it for your future use.

3 TABLESPOONS CINNAMON
2 TABLESPOONS GINGER
1 TEASPOON NUTMEG
½ TEASPOON OF CLOVES AND/OR ALLSPICE

Sift together and store in an airtight jar. *{Makes nearly ¼ cup}*

CHOCOLATE SAUCES

A dribble of chocolate sauce over ice cream or a dishful to dunk a wedge of apple or section of orange into improves dessert nicely. Making your own to have on hand is smart and easy. Two sauce recipes follow: one needs heating to soften it up enough to pour; the other remains soft, pourable.

...

Glorious Chocolate Sauce

The late Karyl Bannister of Southwest Harbor, Maine, a friend and the writer and publisher for many years of *Cook and Tell*, a newsletter dedicated to home cooking, included this recipe in an issue and I adopted it eagerly. Wonderfully rich, a spoonful turns a dish of vanilla ice cream into something worth eating. (I'm not that fond of plain vanilla.)

You can store it in a cupboard, and microwave it briefly to serve. If it becomes too stiff to soften easily, add a little cream or milk to loosen it.

8 TABLESPOONS (1 STICK) BUTTER

14 OUNCES OF SWEETENED CONDENSED MILK

1¾ CUPS LIGHT CORN SYRUP

2 CUPS OR TWELVE OUNCES CHOCOLATE CHIPS

Mix all together in the top of a double boiler over boiling water, whisking until it is smooth. Cook for thirty minutes, stirring often. Store in a jar and reheat in the microwave or by placing the jar in a pan of hot water.

. . .

Kathie's Chocolate Sauce

Sheila Cookson shared this recipe, which she acquired from friend Kathie. Sheila said, "This is a favorite of mine...I don't think it will stiffen in the fridge, although it doesn't last long enough to find out." This is the sauce to make when you need sauce in a hurry. It is quite sweet, and goes together in a flash and remains pourable when cold.

2 CUPS SUGAR

½ CUP COCOA, SIFTED

1 CUP WATER

3 TABLESPOONS WHITE CORN SYRUP

PINCH OF SALT

1 TEASPOON VANILLA

Combine sugar, cocoa, water, corn syrup, and salt, stirring until the mixture is smooth. Bring to a boil, and boil one minute. Remove from the heat and stir in 1 teaspoon vanilla. Use right away or cool and store in a jar. {Makes 2½ cups}

→→→ HOMEMADE SNACKS ←←←

The chip and snack aisle of the average grocery store bulges with ridiculously delicious and hard-to-make at home items. Almost no one I know makes their own potato chips, much less all the variations like barbecue, jalapeno, dill pickle, salt and vinegar, sour cream and onion—you name it, not to mention their equivalents in corn chips, plus popcorns, plus pretzels, and miscellaneous sweet potato, extruded vegetable substances—well, you get the picture. The good news is there are a few really delicious homemade snacks that satisfy the munchies during game day or streaming movies. Then there are cheesy crisps, and crackers that go well with a pre-prandial drink or glass of wine.

· · ·

Party Snack Mix

My former brother-in-law Larry Johnson, who lives in Connecticut, mixes this up during the holidays and sends bagsful to his daughter, Sarah, who shares some with me. It is better than the usual and is reasonably wholesome compared with some of the other junk we pick up as snack food.

LARRY'S PARTY MIX

2 CUPS CORN CHEX

2 CUPS WHEAT CHEX

2 CUPS RICE CHEX

2 CUPS CHEERIOS

2 CUPS MINI SHREDDED WHEATS

2 CUPS PRETZEL STICKS

2 CUPS MIXED NUTS

¾ CUP OR ONE AND A HALF STICKS BUTTER

2 TEASPOONS SEASONING SALT

2 TABLESPOONS WORCESTERSHIRE SAUCE

Heat the oven to 250 degrees. Put all the cereals, pretzels and nuts into a large bowl. Melt the butter, stir in the seasoning salt and Worcestershire and pour over the cereals, tossing to coat the ingredients. Spread them in a thin layer in a large baking pan or two, and bake for forty-five minutes, stirring every fifteen minutes. Cool the mix on paper towels to absorb excess oiliness, and store in a container with tight lid until serving.

{Makes 14 cups of party mix}

{ADVICE}

» You can mix these up, form the dough into variously shaped logs to wrap in waxed paper or plastic, and store them in a plastic bag in the fridge or freezer until you want to bake them. Roll the dough into a round log; flatten all four sides for a square; make rectangles with a flatter lengthwise shape; or triangles by turning the log into a three-sided one. To bake, just slice them off and put them on a baking sheet for only fifteen minutes at 350 degrees! (The edges do soften as they bake, so the shapes will have slightly rounded corners.)

You can, of course, just roll small balls between your palms, and flatten them with a fork on the baking sheet, but then people think they are cookies.

· · ·

CRISPY CHEESY CRACKERS

Homemade cheese crisps, wafers, straws, and crackers recipes abound because butter, cheese, and flour stick together like crazy when baked. Here are two homemade crisps you can assemble for parties or snacking any day.

· · ·

CHEDDAR CRISPS

Years ago, the late, great *Gourmet* magazine offered a recipe for Rice Krispies blended into a flour/cheese/butter mix. I first encountered these crisps at an annual New Year's Eve party thrown by island neighbors Marcy and Bob Congdon and I asked for the recipe. I make a batch every year and give them away at Christmas as private stashes for beloved friends. When baked, the cereal absorbs some of the fat in the cheese which bonds with the sugar in the rice and turns into magical little nuggets of yumminess.

1 POUND SOFTENED BUTTER

1 POUND GRATED SHARP CHEDDAR CHEESE

4 CUPS OF ALL-PURPOSE FLOUR

3 TEASPOONS OF SALT

1 TEASPOON CAYENNE OR OTHER SPICE (OPTIONAL)

4 CUPS CRISPY RICE CEREAL

In a mixer bowl, with a dough hook, beat together the softened butter and the grated cheddar. Toss flour, salt, and spice together in a bowl or put into a sifter, and add to the butter and cheese mixture, continuing to beat. Fold in the crispy rice cereal last and mix until it is blended all through the very stiff dough. Divide the dough and form logs no more than two inches in diameter. Wrap and chill. To bake, heat the oven to 350 degrees. Lightly grease a baking sheet or line with parchment paper. Cut off slices no more than a quarter inch thick and arrange on the baking sheet. Bake for fifteen minutes. Remove and let cool. Store in a tightly sealed container or serve immediately. {Yields dozens and dozens, depending on how large you make them}

CHEESE CRISPS

Ruth Thurston in Machias provided this recipe. The base is like the one in the preceding recipe. She and I have very similar preferences for flavor, so I haven't tinkered much with the spicing for these crisps. If you like spicy, you can zip these crisps up to daredevil levels of heat with red pepper or cayenne, though I substituted chipotle powder, my favorite of all the peppers, for cayenne, and I added a little more dried mustard. A couple of drops of liquid smoke might be a good addition if you have some. I sprinkled a little coarse salt over the top of them, too.

This recipe calls for Rice Chex coarsely crumbled to roll into the top of the crisps. This points to an active little cereal company test kitchen: those folks are always looking for ways to sell you more cereal than you can pour into your family's breakfast bowls. I used the Rice Chex and also tried sesame and poppy seeds.

When working the butter and cheese into the flour and spice mixture, one can use a spoon or even a mixer, but nature provides us with ten fingers that get the job done in about thirty seconds. Before rolling out the dough, I divided it into four parts and formed it into four flattened disks which chill quickly.

2 CUPS OF FLOUR

½ TEASPOON SALT

¼ TEASPOON CAYENNE OR CHILI POWDER

½ TEASPOON DRY MUSTARD

1 CUP (2 STICKS) SOFTENED BUTTER

8 OUNCES GRATED SHARP OR EXTRA-SHARP CHEDDAR (NOT BAGGED)

½ CUP WATER

DASH EACH OF WORCESTERSHIRE AND TABASCO SAUCES

2 CUPS COARSELY CRUMBLED RICE CHEX

Whisk together flour, salt, and spices in a large bowl. Work the softened butter into the flour mixture, then add the grated cheese and mix that in thoroughly. Add the water and Worcestershire and Tabasco, toss all together until the water is taken up. Divide the dough into four parts and make flat disks which you can wrap in waxed paper to chill until they are firm but

{ADVICE}

❰❰ Some like it hot. These cheese crisps call for Tabasco. You can substitute your favorite from the many hot sauces offered these days, some Maine made that, even use soy sauce or tamari.
Messing with the spices doesn't alter the structure of the crackers, so you can use pretty much whatever you like and have on hand. Chili powder, taco seasoning, garlic or onion powder, or barbecue spice mix, whatever goes with cheese, all work.
There is nothing wrong with just plain old salt and pepper, either; if you have coarsely ground black pepper and flaky sea salt, try those.

malleable. Heat the oven to 425 degrees and line baking sheets with parchment paper. Roll the dough until it is about an eighth of an inch thick, sprinkle with the crumbled Rice Chex or you choice of toppings. Roll the topping lightly into the surface of the dough. Cut into squares, rectangles, diamonds—your choice of shapes and sizes—and spread them out on the parchment paper-covered baking sheets. Bake for ten to twelve minutes if you use the Rice Chex or closer to eight minutes if you choose seeds, or just salt and pepper. Aim for a golden color.

Chips, Variations on a Theme

*U*se olive oil to make chips. Before you cut the pita slabs or tortillas into chip-sized pieces, pour a little oil into a saucer, dip the pastry brush into it, and paint them.

At this point, sprinkle pepper, coarse or flaky salt, seasoning salt, garlic, curry, chili, cumin, chipotle powders, paprika, smoked paprika, red pepper flakes, or more exotic spice blends like raz al hanout, za'atar, Lebanese seven-spice blend. For barbecue chips, use a sugary salty barbecue dry rub blend.

If you want to use dried herbs like basil, rosemary, thyme, crumble them very small and whisk them into the olive oil along with salt and pepper before spreading it on the chips.

After they've been oiled and seasoned, cut the pitas into chip-sized pieces. Usually, I lay pitas flat on parchment-lined baking sheets, and for the tortillas, a bare pan, which helps them bake dry.

For pita chips, plain or whole wheat pockets work; make sure they are fresh and fairly moist so they don't fall apart, and use scissors to cut through the perimeter fold. You can cut them into triangles or little rectangles.

Tortillas are easier. Pile up two or three and with a sharp knife, cut wedges any size you like. These produce a hearty chip that doesn't break if you dip into refried beans

Baking them requires attention. You can bake pita chips at 400 degrees and it takes only seven minutes, but watch them closely. Or bake at 375 degrees and check them after five minutes, half-way through baking, then give them another five minutes or so as needed. Tortilla chips take five minutes per side at 400.

...

HOMEMADE CHIPS

Pita and corn chips prepared and bagged or boxed up—and lots of the time, seasoned with every flavor imaginable— wait for us at the grocery store. The container usually holds not many ounces and always a portion of broken bits rest at the bottom, good for sprinkling into soup, or atop salad, or tossed casually into the palm of a hand and thence into an open mouth. I hate to think how much I have spent on these little treats over the years, how much shelf space I have dedicated to storing them.

Each can be a do-it-yourself project, requiring only the pita bread and tortillas they are made out of, so I still have to buy something I probably wouldn't make at home.

...

PITA CHIPS

Use regular sandwich-sized white, whole wheat, or multi-grain pita pockets. Cut them in half by snipping around the perimeter. Oil and season on the inside (rough) surface. Cut into wedges or rectangles. Bake in a single layer on parchment covered baking sheet at 375 for eight to ten minutes or until they are a golden color. You do not need to turn them.

...

TORTILLA CHIPS

Use fresh white or yellow corn tortillas. Oil lightly both sides of a whole tortilla and sprinkle with salt and seasonings. Cut into desired shape and spread in a single layer on an ungreased baking sheet. Bake at 400 for five minutes, then turn them and bake another five minutes or until they are golden.

SIMPLY DONE

. . .

Cinnamon Sugar

Try one part of cinnamon to four parts of sugar, sample, and if you want a more assertive cinnamon flavor, add a shake more; sample again until you get the flavor you prefer. Store in a small jar, preferably one with a shaker top. Never buy premixed cinnamon sugar again.

A couple of hundred years ago, cooks added both cinnamon and ground ginger to sugar to enhance baked goods and fruits. Consider adding a little ginger to your cinnamon sugar, sample, and adjust to your taste.

. . .

Simple Syrup

You can buy simple syrup but since many summer beverages call for it, and it is a standard element for many mixed drinks, why not make your own? Maple syrup, honey, and cane sugar simple syrups are more effective sweeteners for drinks from iced coffee and tea to cocktails than simply stirring in sugar and trying to get it to dissolve.

Cane simple syrups have more flavor when made with turbinado or light brown sugars. Equal parts of sugar and hot water, mixed until the sugar is completely dissolved will keep in a bottle for quite a while in the fridge. Plus, they can be flavored by the addition of spice or citrus to the water and sugar before boiling, then allowed to steep as it cools. Strain out the whole spice, or peel and store the syrup for use.

1 CUP OF WHITE GRANULATED SUGAR

1 CUP WATER

Mix together the water and sugar and heat until the sugar completely dissolves. Let cool. Bottle and refrigerate.

. . .

Homemade Balsamic Vinegar

Real deal balsamic vinegar has been allowed to age for years, is very thick and sweet. And expensive.

To achieve a thicker and sweeter balsamic vinegar, a cooking-school chef advised me to empty a bottle of inexpensive, sharp, and liquid vinegar into a non-reactive saucepan, tand let it evaporate slowly over a low temperature until it coats the back of a spoon. Bottle and use whenever balsamic vinegar is called for.

RECIPE INDEX